go! CHINESE

听说读打写

GO 100

Textbook

(Simplified Character Edition)

罗秋昭
Julie LO

薛意梅
Emily YIH

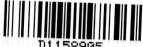

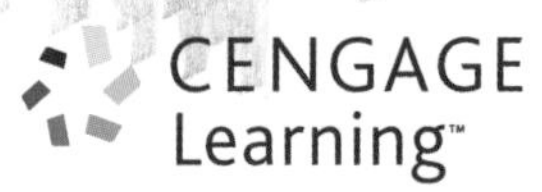

Andover • Melbourne • Mexico City • Stamford, CT • Toronto • Hong Kong • New Delhi • Seoul • Singapore • Tokyo

Go! Chinese Go100 Textbook
(Simplified Character Edition)
Julie Lo, Emily Yih

Publishing Director, CLT Product Director:
Paul K. H. Tan

Editorial Manager:
Lan Zhao

Associate Development Editor:
Coco Koh

Senior Product Manager (Asia):
Joyce Tan

Product Manager (Outside Asia):
Mei Yun Loh

Assistant Publishing Manager:
Pauline Lim

Production Executive:
Cindy Chai

Account Manager (China):
Arthur Sun

Assistant Editor, ELT:
Yuan Ting Soh

ISBN-13: 978-981-4246-42-2
ISBN-10: 981-4246-42-5

Cengage Learning Asia Pte Ltd
5 Shenton Way #01-01
UIC Building
Singapore 068808

Cengage Learning is a leading provider of customized learning solutions with office locations around the globe, including Andover, Melbourne, Mexico City, Stamford (CT), Toronto, Hong Kong, New Delhi, Seoul, Singapore, and Tokyo. Locate your local office at **www.cengage.com/global**

Cengage Learning products are represented in Canada by Nelson Education, Ltd.

For product information, visit **www.cengagesasia.com**

Photo credits:
Cover: © Getty Images. p.28: (left to right) 31210800, 36107311, 23299479, 231420920, 2701148 © Jupiterimages Corporation; p.38: 36107095 © Jupiterimages Corporation.

Printed in Singapore
4 5 6 7 14 13 12 11

Acknowledgements

Go! Chinese is designed to be used together with ***IQChinese Go*** courseware, a series of multimedia CD-ROM developed by **IQChinese**. We sincerely thank **Wu, Meng-Tien** (Instruction Manager, IQChinese) and **Lanni Wang** (Instruction Specialist, IQChinese) for their tremendous editorial support and advice throughout the development of this program.

We also like to thank the following individuals who offered many helpful insights, ideas, and suggestions for improvement during the product development stage of ***Go! Chinese***.

- **Jessie Lin Brown**, Singapore American School, Singapore
- **Henny Chen**, Moreau Catholic High School, USA
- **Yeafen Chen**, University of Wisconsin-Milwaukee, USA
- **Christina Hsu**, Superior Education, USA
- **Yi Liang Jiang**, Beijing Language and Culture University, China
- **Yan Jin**, Singapore American School, Singapore
- **Kerman Kwan**, Irvine Chinese School, USA
- **Andrew Scrimgeour**, University of South Australia, Australia
- **James L. Tan**, Grace Christian High School, the Philippines
- **Man Tao**, Koning Williem I College, the Netherlands
- **Chiungwen Tsai**, Westside Chinese School, USA
- **Tina Wu**, Westside High School, USA
- **YaWen (Alison) Yang**, Concordian International School, Thailand

Preface

Go! Chinese, together with ***IQChinese Go* multimedia CD-ROM**, is a fully-integrated Chinese language program that offers an easy, enjoyable, and effective learning experience for learners of Chinese as a foreign language.

The themes and lesson plans of the program are designed with reference to the American National Standards for Foreign Language Learning developed by ACTFL[1], and the Curriculum Guides for Modern Languages developed by the Toronto District Board of Education. The program aims to help beginners develop their communicative competence in the four language skills of listening, speaking, reading, and writing while gaining an appreciation of the Chinese culture, exercising their ability to compare and contrast different cultures, making connections with other discipline areas, and extending their learning experiences to their home and communities.

The program employs innovative teaching methodologies and computer applications to enhance language learning, as well as keep students motivated in and outside of the classroom. The CD-ROM companion gives students access to audio, visual, and textual information about the language all at once. Chinese typing is systematically integrated into the program to facilitate the acquisition and retention of new vocabulary and to equip students with a skill that is becoming increasingly important in the Internet era wherein more and more professional and personal correspondence are done electronically.

Course Design

The program is divided into two series: Beginner and Intermediate. The Beginner Series, which comprises four levels (Go100-400), provides a solid foundation for continued study of the Intermediate Series (Go500-800). Each level includes a student text, a workbook, and a CD-ROM companion.

Beginner Series: Go100 – Go400

Designed for zero beginners, each level of the Beginner Series is made up of 10 colorfully illustrated lessons. Each lesson covers new vocabulary and simple sentence structures with particular emphasis on listening and speaking skills. In keeping with the communicative approach, a good mix of activities such as role play, interviews, games, pair work, and language exchanges are incorporated to allow students to learn to communicate through interaction in the target language. The CD-ROM uses rhythmic chants, word games, quizzes, and Chinese typing exercises to improve students' pronunciation, mastery of *pinyin*, and their ability to recognize and read words and sentences taught in each lesson.

The Beginner Series can be completed in roughly 240 hours (160 hours on Textbook and 80 hours on CD-ROM). Upon completion of the Beginner Series, the student will have acquired approximately 500 Chinese characters and 1000 common phrases.

Intermediate Series: Go500 – Go800

The Intermediate Series continues with the use of the communicative approach, but places a greater emphasis on Culture, Community, and Comparison. Through stories revolving around Chinese-American families, students learn vocabulary necessary for expressing themselves in a variety of contexts, describing their world, and discussing cultural differences.

The Intermediate Series can be completed in roughly 320 hours (240 hours on Textbook and 80 hours on CD-ROM). Upon completion of both the Beginner and Intermediate Series, the student will have acquired approximately 1000 Chinese characters and 2400 common phrases.

[1] American Council on the Teaching of Foreign Languages (http://www.actfl.org)

Course Features

Vocabulary and Sentence Structures

The program places emphasis on helping students use the target language in contexts relevant to their everyday lives. Therefore, the chosen vocabulary and sentence structures are based on familiar topics such as family, school activities, hobbies, weather, shopping, food, pets, modes of transport, etc. The same topics are revisited throughout the series to reinforce learning, as well as to expand on the vocabulary and sentence structures acquired before.

Listening and Speaking

Communicative activities encourage and require a learner to speak with and listen to other learners. Well-designed and well-executed communicative activities can help turn the language classroom into an active and enjoyable place where learners are motivated to learn and can learn what they need. The program integrates a variety of communicative activities such as role play, interviews, games, pair work, and language exchanges to give students the opportunity to put what they have learned into practice.

Word Recognition and Reading

Each lesson introduces about 12 new Chinese characters. Using the spiral approach, each new character is first introduced and then recycled in classroom activities and subsequent lessons to enhance retention of new vocabulary over time. *Pinyin* (phonetic notation) is added above newly introduced characters so that students can learn to pronounce them. To make sure students do not become over-reliant on *pinyin* to read Chinese, recycled vocabulary is stripped of *pinyin* so that students can learn to recognize and read the actual written characters in due course. For the same reason, the CD-ROM companion does not display the *pinyin* of words automatically.

Type-to-Learn Methodology

The unique characteristic of this series is the use of Chinese typing as an instructional strategy to improve listening, pronunciation, and word recognition. Activities in the CD-ROM require students to type characters or sentences as they are read aloud or displayed on the computer screen. Students will be alerted if they make a mistake and will be given the chance to correct them. If they do not get it right on the third try, the software provides immediate feedback on how to correct the error. This interactive trial-and-error method allows students to develop self-confidence and learn the language by doing.

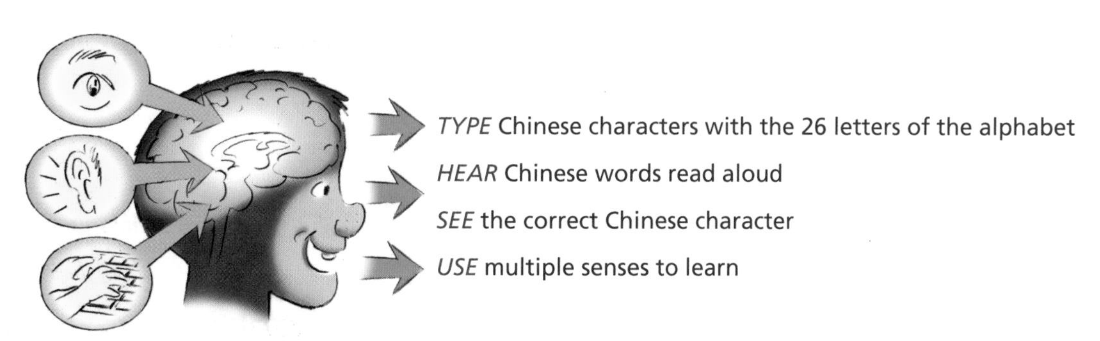
TYPE Chinese characters with the 26 letters of the alphabet
HEAR Chinese words read aloud
SEE the correct Chinese character
USE multiple senses to learn

Chinese Characters and Character Writing

The program does not require the student to be able to hand-write all the core vocabulary; the teacher may however assign more character writing practice according to his or her classroom emphasis and needs. What the program aims to do is to give students a good grasp of Chinese radicals and stroke order rules, as well as to help students understand and appreciate the characteristics and formation of Chinese characters. The program includes writing practice on frequently used characters. Understanding the semantic function radicals have in the characters they form and having the ability to see compound characters by their simpler constituents enable students to memorize new characters in a logical way.

Using the CD-ROM as an Instructional Aid

The following diagram shows how a teacher might use the CD-ROM as an instructional aid to improve traditional classroom instruction.

	Textbook	*CD-ROM*

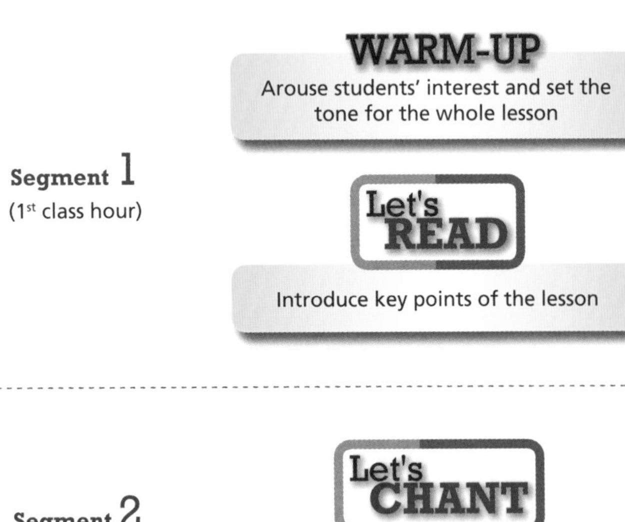

Text > Chant

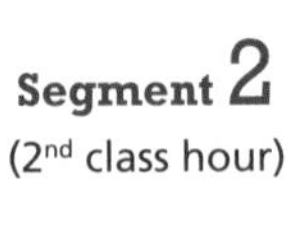

Rhyming text to be read aloud

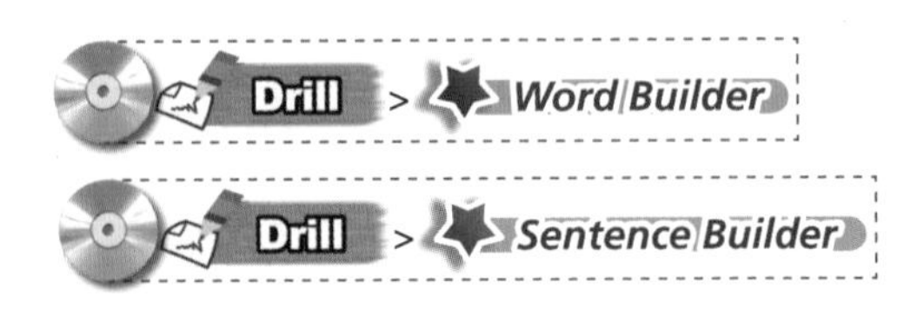

Segment 4
(4th class hour)

Segment 5
(5th class hour)

Scripted dialogue practice that may be extended or modified

Let's DO IT

Review and reinforcement activities

Segment 6
(6th class hour)

LEARNING LOG

Conclusion and students' self-evaluation

#Sentence Quiz Exercise

The section *Exercise > Sentence Quiz* in the CD-ROM enhances learning by stimulating multiple senses and providing immediate feedback on students' performance.

The Sentence Quiz exercise comprises four levels.

- Level 1 – Warm-up Quiz (Look, Listen, and Type): Chinese text, *pinyin*, and audio prompts are provided.
- Level 2 – Visual-aid Quiz: Only Chinese text is provided. There are no *pinyin* or audio prompts.
- Level 3 – Audio-aid Quiz: Only audio prompts are provided.
- Level 4 – Character-selection Quiz: Only Chinese text is provided. After entering the correct *pinyin*, students are required to select the correct character from a list of similar-looking characters.

Classroom Setup and Equipment

FFor small classes (up to 5 students), the teacher can show the CD-ROM features on one computer with students gathered around the screen. For large groups, a projector will be needed to project the computer's display onto a large screen so that the entire class can see.

If the classroom is not equipped with computers, the teacher may have students bring their own portable computers to class so that they can work individually or in small groups of 2 to 3 on the CD-ROM activities during designated class hours. CD-ROM activities may also be assigned as homework.

Suggestions for Teachers

We recommend that the teachers

- be flexible in using the *pinyin* unit. They may, for example, extend the *pinyin* exercise to an enunciation exercise based on the lesson's theme and new vocabulary. They may also choose to use the *pinyin* unit as an introductory exercise before embarking on the first lesson of the series.
- spend 4-5 hours on each lesson in the Textbook and 2 hours on each lesson in the CD-ROM. The course materials and lesson length may be adjusted according to students' proficiency level and learning ability.
- allocate 1-2 class hours to go over with students the Review units in the Workbook as a way to check on the students' progress.
- have students complete 1-2 pages of the Workbook after every two class sessions.
- encourage students to spend 10 minutes a day on the Sentence Quiz in the CD-ROM. Practice makes perfect!

For detailed chapter-by-chapter lesson plans, teaching slides, and supplementary assignments, please refer to one of the following websites:

Cengage Learning http://www.cengageasia.com

IQChinese http://www.iqchinese.com

Scope & Sequence

Lesson	Communicative Goals	Vocabulary	Language Usage	Cultural Information
一二三 One Two Three 1	• Count up to 100 • Indicate the count of an item	**Numbers 1 to 100** 一, 二…十, 百, 两, 个	• **Usage of "二" and "两"** 二十, 两百, 一千二百 • **Measure word "个"** 一个, 两个	
你好吗? How Are You? 2	• Greet people in different situations • Ask how someone is doing	**Greetings** 你, 我, 他, 你们, 大家, 好, 吗, 很, 早, 再见…	• **Personal pronouns** 你, 我, 他 • **Plural form of personal pronouns** 我们, 你们, 他们 • **Modulation of third-tone words** 你好, 你早, 很好 • **Interrogative sentence with "吗"** 你好吗?	• How Chinese people greet one another
谢谢你! Thank You! 3	• Express and respond to a thank-you • Express and respond to an apology	**Thanks and Apologies** 谢谢, 不客气, 对不起, 没关系, 请, 不用…	• **Usage of "谢谢" and "不客气"** 谢谢大家, 请不用客气 • **Adverb "不" and negative form** 不好, 不对, 不用谢	• Chinese characters with left/right components • Chinese radicals
姓什么? What Is Your Last Name? 4	• Ask for someone's name • Tell your name • Introduce others	**Exchanging Names** 请问, 贵姓, 叫, 什么, 的, 名字, 都…	• **Difference between "姓", "名", and "名字"** 你叫什么名字? 我姓谢, 叫小明。 • **Possessive form "的"** 我的名字。 • **Interrogative pronoun "什么"** 你姓什么? 你叫什么名字? • **Polite form "请问" when asking questions** 请问你贵姓?	• Chinese names • Common Chinese last names
星期几? What Day Is Today? 5	• Express days of the week • Express day, month, and year • Ask and answer questions about dates • Tell the number of days between two given dates	**Dates, months, weeks, years** 星期, 日, 月, 天, 今年, 明年, 去年, 今天, 明天, 昨天, 有, 没有, 到, 是, 几, 这个…	• **How to express dates** 今天是二〇〇九年七月十六日星期四。 • **"是" Sentence** 请问今天是几月几日? • **Usage of "到"** 四月一日到四月二十日有二十天。 • **Sentence pattern "有 / 没有"** 一个星期有七天。 二月没有三十日。 • **Usage of "这个"** 这个月有几个星期?	• Early Chinese writing system: pictograms • Chinese characters with top/bottom components

几口人? How Many People Are There in Your Family? **6**	• Introduce your family members • Ask about someone's family members • Ask and answer simple yes/no questions	**The Family** 爸爸, 妈妈, 哥哥, 弟弟, 姐姐, 妹妹, 还有, 一共, 人, 口, 家…	• **Measure word "口"** 请问你家几口人? • **Sentence patterns "有 / 没有 / 有……吗?/ 有没有……?"** 你有妹妹吗? 我有（没有）妹妹。 • **Sentence patterns "有……, 还有……"** 我有姐姐，还有妹妹。 • **Yes/No questions** 你没有哥哥吗? 对，我没有哥哥。	• How to address family members in Chinese
多少钱? How Much Is This? **7**	• Ask what someone wants to buy • Tell someone what you want to buy • Ask for and state the price of an item • Ask for a lower price	**Shopping** 钱, 块, 要, 买, 那个, 太, 贵, 便宜, 算, 一点儿, 多少…	• **Usage of "这个 / 那个"** 那个十块钱。 • **Opposites "便宜 / 贵" and "少 / 多"** 27块太贵了，便宜一点儿好不好? • **Adverb of degree "很"** 很大, 很小 • **Sentence patterns "要 / 要……吗?"** 你要买裙子吗? 我不买裙子，我要买鞋子。 • **Usage of "多少 / 几"** 请问这个多少钱? 你几岁?	
几点钟? What Time Is It? **8**	• Tell and ask for the time • Ask and tell if someone will be at a certain location at a certain time	**Time Expressions** 点, 分, 半, 钟, 上午, 中午, 下午, 晚上, 现在, 时, 走, 分钟…	• **How to tell time** 请问现在几点（钟）? 现在中午十二点三十五分。 • **Sentence patterns "在 / 不在 / 在……吗?/ 在不在?"** 明天你在不在家?	
打电话 Making a Phone Call **9**	• Conduct basic telephone conversations • Inquire and tell your telephone number	**Phone Conversation** 打电话, 号, 找, 哪一位, 等, 谁, 来…	• **Usage of "谁"** 请问你找谁? • **Sentence patterns "是 / 不是 / 是……吗?"** 他是谢小明吗? 不是，他是小明的哥哥。 • **Usage of " 等 / 等一下 / 等一等"** 请你等一等（等一下）。 请你等十分钟。 • **Difference between "那" and "哪"** 哪一位是小明的爸爸? 那位是小明的爸爸。	• Common practice of Chinese people when making or answering phone calls • Chinese radicals
好老师 A Good Teacher **10**	• Talk about abilities • Address a teacher politely	**Abilities** 老师, 同学, 教, 学, 中文, 会, 可以, 和, 学生, 有用, 一起…	• **Sentence patterns "会 / 不会 / 会……吗?"** 你会中文吗? 我会中文。 • **Sentence patterns "可以 / 不可以 / 可以……吗?"** 我可以打电话吗? 你不可以打电话。	• Chinese refers to someone by their titles as a show of respect for age and hierarchy

Table of Contents

Pinyin

Pinyin consists of three parts:

Initial + Final + Tone

Initial	b p m f		d t n l		
	g k h		j q x		
	zh ch sh r		z c s		
Final	a	ai	ao	an	ang
	o	ou			
	e	ei	en	eng	er
	yi (~i)	ya (~ia)	yao (~iao)	yan (~ian)	yang (~iang)
	yo	you (~iu)	ye (~ie)	yin (~in)	ying (~ing)
	wu (~u)	wa (~ua)	wai (~uai)	wan (~uan)	wang (~uang)
	wo (~uo)	wei (~ui)	wen (~un)	weng (~ong)	
	yu (~ü)	yuan (~üan)	yue (~üe)	yun (~ün)	yong (~iong)
Tone	¯ 1	ˊ 2	ˇ 3	ˋ 4	

a o e i u ü

	a	o	e	i	u	ü
b	ba	bo		bi	bu	
m	ma	mo	me	mi	mu	
n	na		ne	ni	nu	nü
l	la		le	li	lu	lü

There are four tones in *pinyin*:

Tone	Tone Mark
1st	ˉ
2nd	ˊ
3rd	ˇ
4th	ˋ

mā má mǎ mà
lī lí lǐ lì
nū nú nǔ nù

bàba

māma

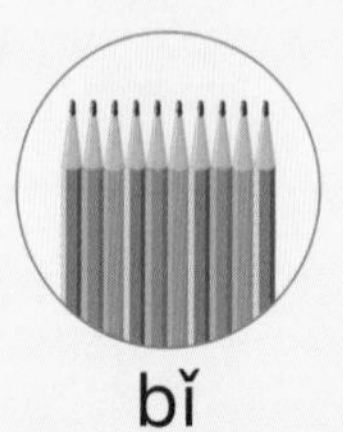
bǐ

lù

nánshēng

nǚshēng

lǜsè

ai ao an ang ei en eng er ou

	ai	ao	an	ang
d	dai	dao	dan	dang
t	tai	tao	tan	tang

dàngāo

	ei	en	eng
p	pei	pen	peng
f	fei	fen	feng

er

táng

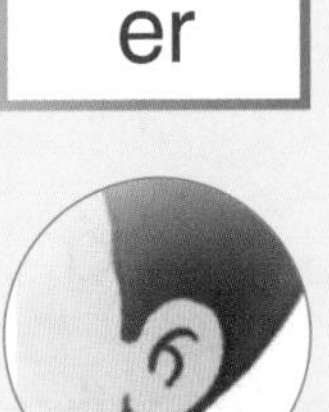

ěrduo

	ou
g	gou
k	kou
h	hou

mìfēng

gǒu

āi ái ǎi ài

kōu kóu kǒu kòu

mēi méi měi mèi

huī huí huǐ huì

liū liú liǔ liù

Memorize It

The basic rule for placing the tone mark:

Mark "a" if you see "a",

Mark "o" or "e" when there's no "a",

And when "u" and "i" are side by side,

Mark the one that comes last.

i	u	ü
yi	wu	yu

When Finals "i", "u", and "ü" make syllables themselves without any Initials, they are written differently. For example:

yi	yī	yí	yǐ	yì	~i
ya		yá	yǎ	yà	~ia
yao	yāo	yáo	yǎo		~iao
yan	yān	yán	yǎn	yàn	~ian
yang	yāng		yǎng	yàng	~iang
yo	yō	yó	yǒ	yò	
you	yōu	yóu	yǒu	yòu	~i(o)u
ye	yē	yé	yě	yè	~ie
yin	yīn	yín	yǐn	yìn	~in
ying	yīng	yíng	yǐng	yìng	~ing

diàndēng

niúnǎi

shǒubiǎo

yǎnjing

miàn

xiāngjiāo

jīnyú

wu	wū	wú	wǔ	wù	~u
wa	wā	wá	wǎ	wà	~ua
wai	wāi	wái	wǎi	wài	~uai
wan	wān	wán	wǎn	wàn	~uan
wang	wāng	wáng	wǎng	wàng	~uang
wo	wō	wó		wò	~uo
wei	wēi	wéi	wěi	wèi	~u(e)i
wen	wēn	wén	wěn	wèn	~u(e)n
weng	wēng	wéng	wěng	wèng	~ong

yu	yū		yǔ	yù	~ü
yuan	yuān	yuán	yuǎn	yuàn	~üan
yue	yuē	yué	yuě	yuè	~üe
yun	yūn		yǔn	yùn	~ü(e)n
yong	yōng	yóng	yǒng	yòng	~iong

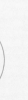

huǒchē

wūguī

huāduǒ

bǐtǒng

lúnzi

yuèliang

yuánquān

xuésheng

chuán

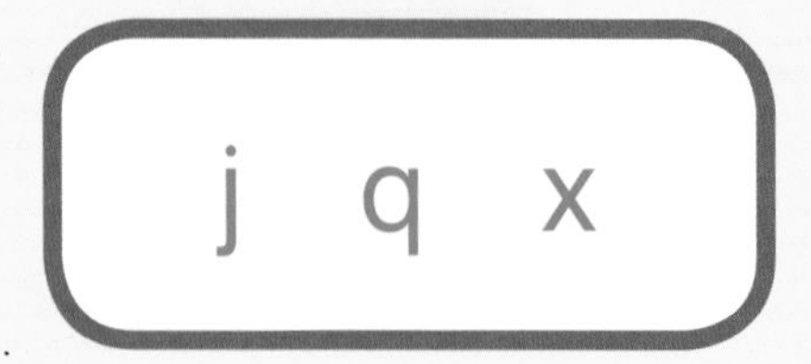

The Finals "iou", "uei", and "uen" should be written as "iu", "ui", and "un" when they are used with an Initial. For example, "niú", "guī", "lún".

	~i	~ia	~ian	~i(o)u	~ü	~ü(e)n	~iong
j	ji	jia	jian	jiu	ju	jun	jiong
q	qi	qia	qian	qiu	qu	qun	qiong
x	xi	xia	xian	xiu	xu	xun	xiong

The Final "ü" should be written as "u" when it is used with the initials "j", "q", and "x".

xiàxuě

xiǎojī

xióng

qián

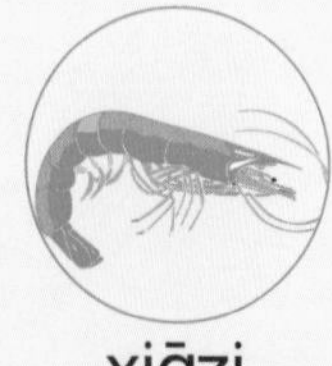
xiāzi

qiáo

zh	ch	sh	r	z	c	s
zhi	chi	shi	ri	zi	ci	si

When the Initials "zh", "ch", "sh", "r", "z", "c", and "s" are pronounced alone, they should be written as "zhi", "chi", "shi", "ri", "zi", "ci", and "si".

	ai	e	eng	~u(e)i	~uan	~ong
zh	zhai	zhe	zheng	zhui	zhuan	zhong
ch	chai	che	cheng	chui	chuan	chong
sh	shai	she	sheng	shui	shuan	
r		re	reng	rui	ruan	
z	zai	ze	zeng	zui	zuan	zong
c	cai	ce	ceng	cui	cuan	cong
s	sai	se	seng	sui	suan	song

zhīzhū

shūbāo

shīzi

shízhōng

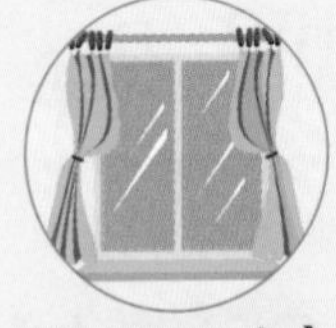
chuānghù

shūcài

Check out the Pinyin CD.

Let's DO IT

1. Mark the third tone on the *pinyin* and read out the words.

2. Listen carefully to your teacher. Which item is mentioned?

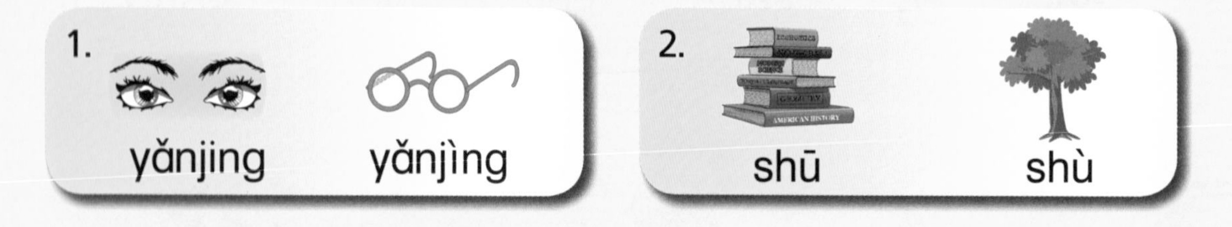

3. Read the sentences.

1. Zǐsè de zhīzhū yǒu jǐ zhī?

2. Gēge kě le hē kělè.

3. Yéye yǒu liù tóu niú.

4. Qī ge qìqiú bǎng yìqǐ.

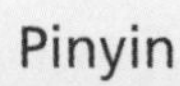

LESSON 1

一二三 One Two Three

My Goals

1 Count in Chinese
2 Express the quantity of an item in Chinese
3 Recognize and write Chinese numbers

Let's READ

1	2	3	4	5
yī	èr	sān	sì	wǔ
一	二	三	四	五

yī èr
一二
yī èr sān
一二三
yī èr sān
一二三
sān èr yī
三二一
yī èr sān sì wǔ
一二三四五
wǔ sì sān èr yī
五四三二一
1
2
3
4
5

New Words

yī
一 one

èr
二 two

sān
三 three

sì
四 four

wǔ
五 five

6	7	8	9	10
liù	qī	bā	jiǔ	shí
六	七	八	九	十

yī èr sān　sān èr yī
一二三　三二一

yī èr sān sì wǔ liù qī
一二三四五六七

qī bā jiǔ　bā jiǔ shí
七八九　八九十

qī liù wǔ sì sān èr yī
七六五四三二一

New Words

liù
六 six

qī
七 seven

bā
八 eight

jiǔ
九 nine

shí
十 ten

Memorize It

Look closely at the roulette and memorize the Chinese numbers 1 to 10.

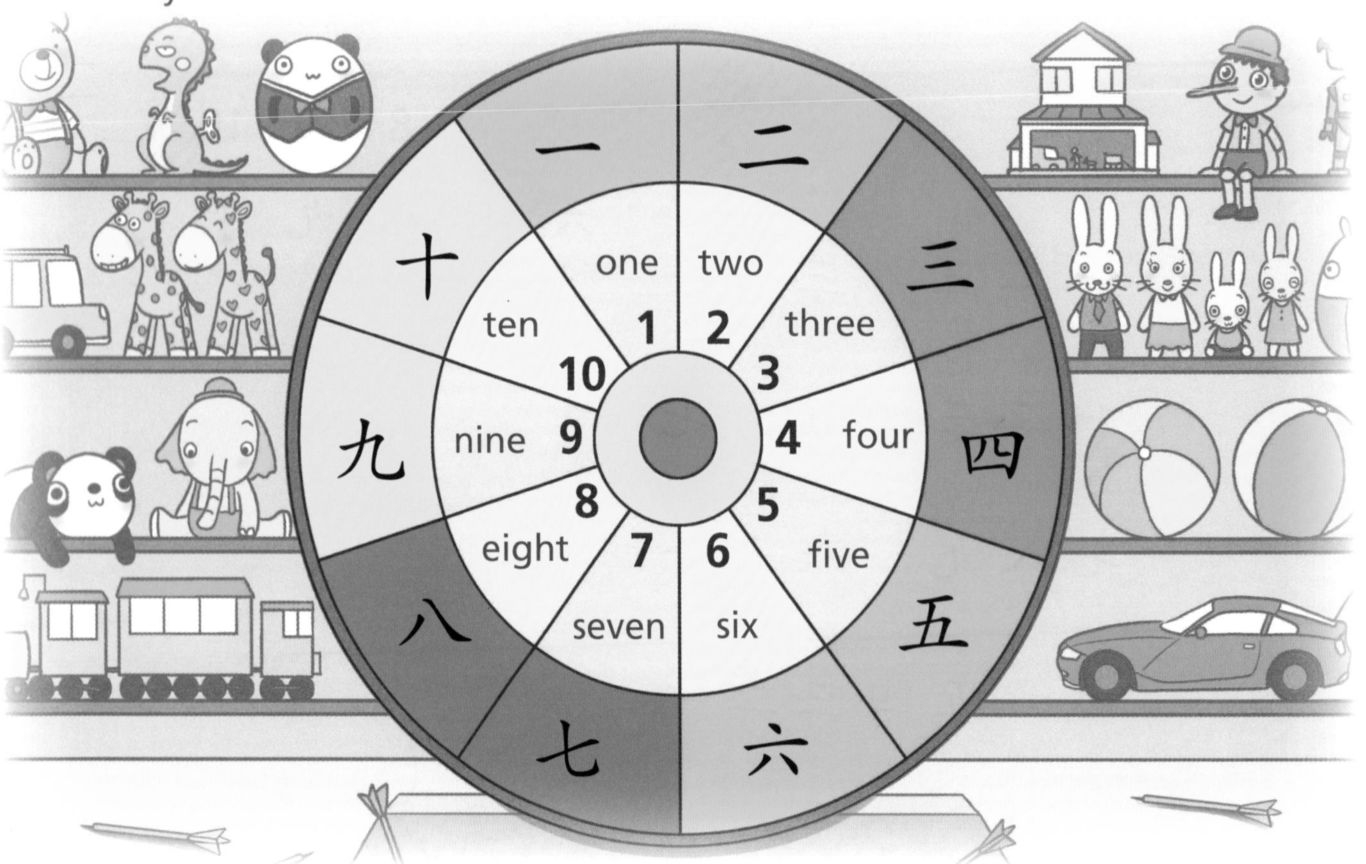

Match and Write

Match each number with its corresponding Chinese character. Then fill in the box with the missing Chinese number.

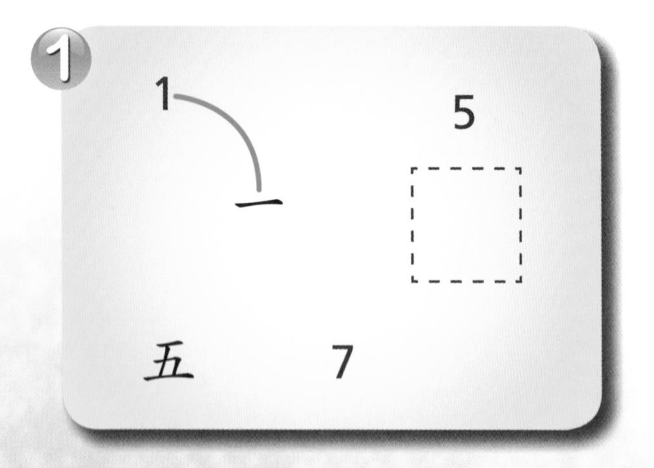

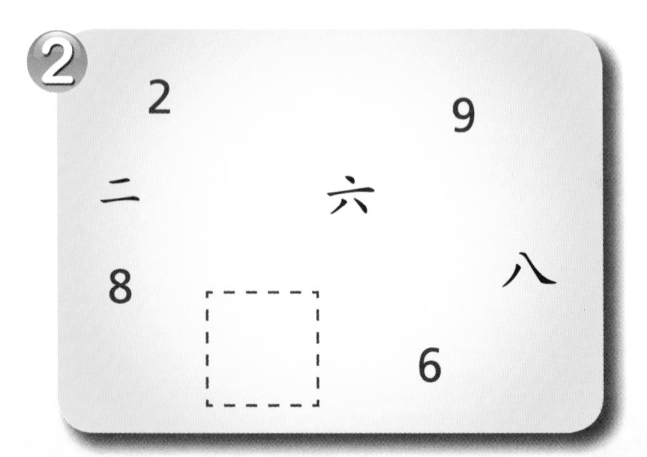

Count from 1 to 100 in Chinese.

	yī 一	èr 二	sān 三	sì 四	wǔ 五	liù 六	qī 七	bā 八	jiǔ 九
shí 十	shí yī 十一		shí sān 十三		shí wǔ 十五		shí qī 十七		shí jiǔ 十九
èr shí 二十		èr shí èr 二十二		èr shí sì 二十四		èr shí liù 二十六		èr shí bā 二十八	
sān shí 三十		sān shí èr 三十二			sān shí wǔ 三十五		sān shí qī 三十七		sān shí jiǔ 三十九
sì shí 四十			sì shí sān 四十三			sì shí liù 四十六			sì shí jiǔ 四十九
wǔ shí 五十	wǔ shí yī 五十一		wǔ shí sān 五十三		wǔ shí wǔ 五十五		wǔ shí qī 五十七		
liù shí 六十		liù shí èr 六十二		liù shí sì 六十四				liù shí bā 六十八	
qī shí 七十	qī shí yī 七十一			qī shí sì 七十四			qī shí qī 七十七		qī shí jiǔ 七十九
bā shí 八十	bā shí yī 八十一				bā shí wǔ 八十五			bā shí bā 八十八	
jiǔ shí 九十		jiǔ shí èr 九十二		jiǔ shí sì 九十四		jiǔ shí liù 九十六			jiǔ shí jiǔ 九十九
yì bǎi 一百									

New Words

bǎi
百 hundred

yī èr sān sì wǔ liù qī
一二三四五六七。

qī liù wǔ sì sān èr yī
七六五四三二一。

bā shí jiǔ shí yì liǎng bǎi
八十、九十、一两百。

"一两百" means 100 and 200.

liù bǎi qī bǎi bā jiǔ bǎi
六百、七百、八九百。

"八九百" means 800 and 900.

New Words

liǎng
两 two

Let's Learn GRAMMAR

0
líng

1	2	3	4	5	6	7	8	9
yī	èr	sān	sì	wǔ	liù	qī	bā	jiǔ
一	二	三	四	五	六	七	八	九

shí
十

10	20	30	40	50
shí	èr shí	sān shí	sì shí	wǔ shí
十	二十	三十	四十	五十
60	70	80	90	
liù shí	qī shí	bā shí	jiǔ shí	
六十	七十	八十	九十	

bǎi
百

100	200	300	400	500
yì bǎi	liǎng bǎi	sān bǎi	sì bǎi	wǔ bǎi
一百	两百	三百	四百	五百
600	700	800	900	
liù bǎi	qī bǎi	bā bǎi	jiǔ bǎi	
六百	七百	八百	九百	

Both "二" and "两" mean "two", but their usage differs.

❶ We use "两" before a measure word and noun. For example:

liǎng ge péng you
两个朋友 (two friends)

liǎng ge nǚ shēng
两个女生 (two girls)

❷ When counting, "二" must always be used before "十". For example: 二十 (twenty)

❸ When combined with "百", the position of the word affects the usage.

➤ If it is placed at the beginning, we usually say "两百" (two hundred), although "二百" is also acceptable.

➤ If it is placed in the middle, we usually use "二". For example:

qiān
一千二百二十 (One thousand, two hundred, and twenty)

Let's SING A SONG

shí ge hǎo péng you

十个好朋友

‖ 1 1 1 1 | 3 5 33 1 |
yí ge liǎng ge sān ge hǎo péng you
一个两个三个好朋友*，

| 2 2 2 2 | 7̣ 2 7̣7̣ 5̣ |
sì ge wǔ ge liù ge hǎo péng you
四个五个六个好朋友，

| 1 1 1 1 | 3 5 33 1 |
qī ge bā ge jiǔ ge hǎo péng you
七个八个九个好朋友，

| 2 2 5̣ 5̣ | 1 - - - ‖
shí ge hǎo péng you
十个好朋友。

*好朋友 good friend

TIP

A measure word is used to quantify objects or people (noun). Different nouns require different measure words. "个" is the most commonly used.

		numeral	measure word	noun
Chinese:	我有	两	个	好朋友。
English:	I have	two		good friends.

New Words

ge
个 (a measure word, used with objects and people)

Read Aloud

yí ge
一个

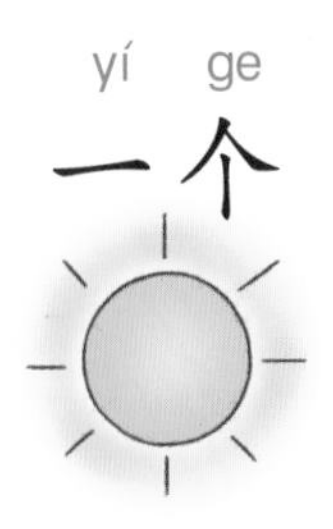

liǎng ge
两个

sān ge
三个

sì ge
四个

wǔ ge
五个

liù ge
六个

qī ge
七个

bā ge
八个

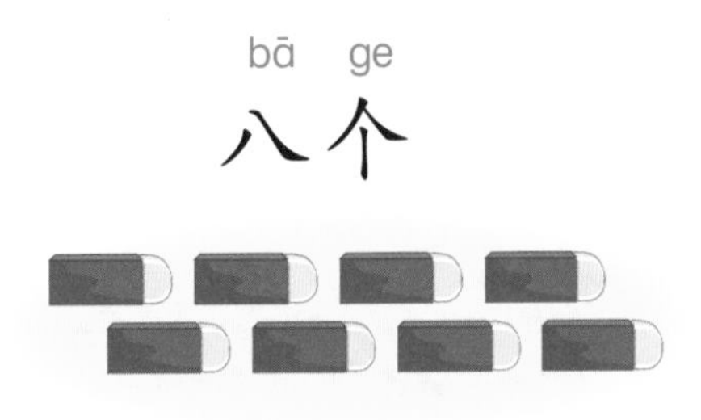

jiǔ ge
九个

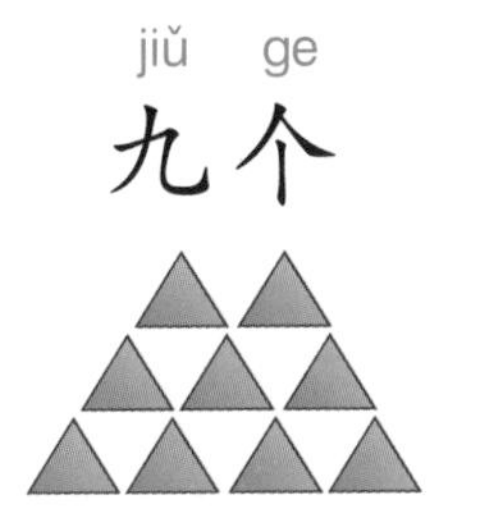

shí ge
十个

Think and Answer

Fill in the blanks with the appropriate Chinese number and measure word "个".

1. How many good friends do you have?

wǒ yǒu ______ hǎo péng you
我有______好朋友。

2. How many boys and girls are there in your class?

bān shàng yǒu ______ nán shēng ______ nǚ shēng
班上有______男生、______女生。

Let's DO IT

Look for the pattern in the charts below. Then write the correct Chinese numbers in the spaces provided.

1

	七十四			七十七	七十八	
			八十三		八十一	
			八十七	八十八		
			九十四			九十一
				九十五	九十六	
					九十九	九十八
						一百

2

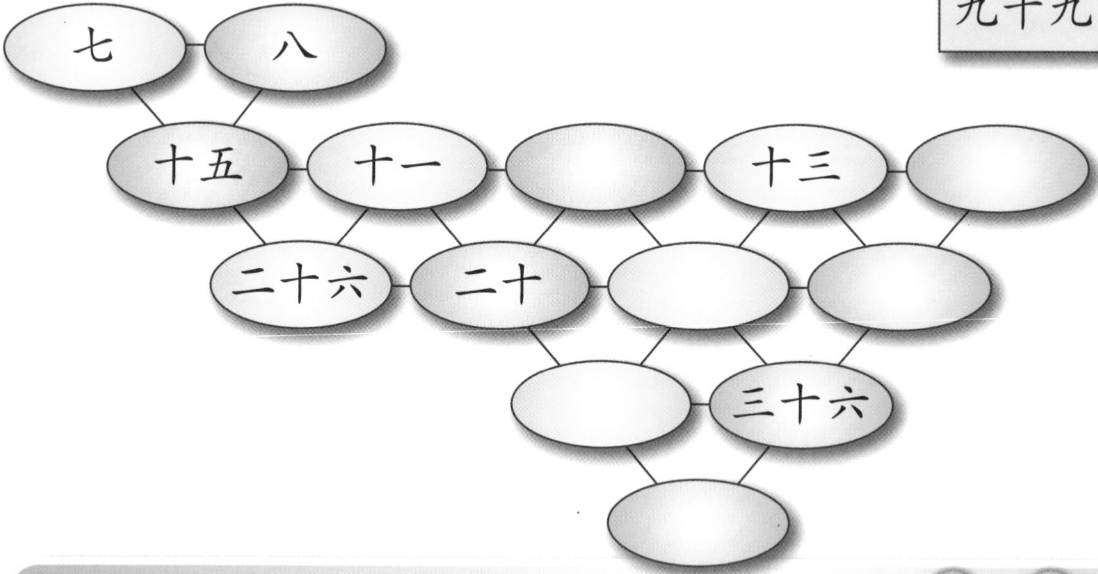

七 — 八

十五 — 十一 — ___ — 十三 — ___

二十六 — 二十 — ___ — ___

___ — 三十六

___

LEARNING LOG

I can...

		Excellent	Good	Fair	Needs Improvement
1	count from 1 to 100 in Chinese.	☐	☐	☐	☐
2	combine the numbers one to nine with "百" to derive one hundred, two hundred, etc.	☐	☐	☐	☐
3	tell the difference between "二" and "两" and use them correctly.	☐	☐	☐	☐
4	understand that the measure word "个" is commonly used to quantify objects or people.	☐	☐	☐	☐
5	write the numbers "一" to "十" in Chinese.	☐	☐	☐	☐

LESSON

2

你好吗？
How Are You?

My Goals

1 Use appropriate greetings when meeting other people in various situations
2 Respond appropriately to greetings from other people
3 Understand how Chinese people greet each other
4 Recognize and write simple vocabulary associated with greetings

TIP Besides verbal greetings, Chinese people also use some common gestures or actions to greet each other, such as waving or shaking hands, smiling, and nodding their heads. How do you usually greet your friends?

New Words

nǐ 你 you (singular)	hǎo 好 fine; good	zǎo 早 early; morning
nǐ zǎo 你早 Good morning (to you)		nǐ hǎo 你好 hello

Use "们" if you are referring to two or more people.

New Words

tā 他 he	wǒ 我 I	wǒ men 我们 we
nǐ men 你们 you (plural)	tā men 他们 they	dà jiā 大家 everybody

nǐ hǎo ma
你好吗？

wǒ hěn hǎo
我很好。

tā hǎo ma
他好吗？

tā hěn hǎo
他很好！

nǐ zǎo nǐ zǎo dà jiā zǎo
你早！你早！大家早！

nǐ hǎo nǐ hǎo dà jiā hǎo
你好！你好！大家好！

ma
吗 (used when asking a question)

hěn
很 very

Let's Learn GRAMMAR

zǎo
早

hǎo
好

nǐ zǎo
你早

dà jiā zǎo
大家早

nǐ hǎo
你好

tā hěn hǎo
他很好

wǒ hěn hǎo
我很好

我	wǒ
早	zǎo
好	hǎo
你	nǐ
很	hěn

nǐ zǎo
你早

hěn hǎo
很好

nǐ hǎo
你好

TIP

When two third tones occur together, the preceding word should be pronounced in the second tone. Look at the examples above and circle the words you pronounced in the second tone.

ma
吗?

hǎo
好

hǎo ma
好吗?

tā hǎo ma
他好吗?

hǎo ma
Tom 好吗?

tā hǎo ma
Jeff 他好吗?

TIP

"吗?" is an essential component in the interrogative sentence structure. It always appears at the end of a question.

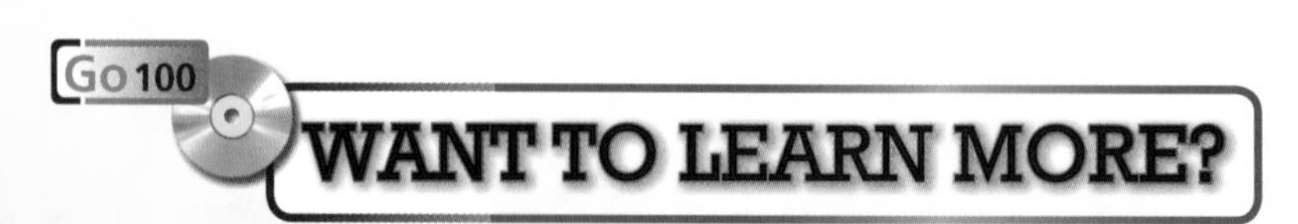

Check out the Text > Sentence Pattern section in the Go100 CD.

Find a partner and practice the dialogues below.

nǐ hǎo
Tom，你好！
nǐ hǎo
Julie，你好！
tā hǎo ma
Jeff 他好吗？
tā hěn hǎo
他很好！

Task 2

A：你好！(nǐ hǎo)

B：你好！(nǐ hǎo)

A：你好吗？(nǐ hǎo ma)

B：我很好。(wǒ hěn hǎo)

Find partners to practice the dialogues below.

Task 3

A: nǐ men hǎo ma
你们好吗？

B C: wǒ men hěn hǎo
我们很好！

Task 4

A: dà jiā zǎo
大家早！

B C D E: nǐ zǎo
你早！

Go100

WANT TO LEARN MORE?

Check out the Text > Dialogue section in the Go100 CD.

Task 5

A: 再见！(zài jiàn)

B: 再见！(zài jiàn)

New Words

再见 (zài jiàn) goodbye

Bye-bye 再见，
bye-bye 再见，
see you again!

Let's DO IT

How do you greet the people in the following situations? Working in pairs, role-play each of the scenarios below.

Scenario 1 You run into your friend outside the classroom in the morning.

Scenario 2 You bump into your old friend, Adam, on the street. You have not seen each other for a long time and wonder how he and his sister, Mary, are doing.

Scenario 3 You run into your classmates who have gathered outside the school library. You are on your way home and bid them goodbye.

LEARNING LOG

I can...	Excellent	Good	Fair	Needs Improvement
1 exchange simple greetings politely in Chinese.	☐	☐	☐	☐
2 ask how someone is doing.	☐	☐	☐	☐
3 reply when someone asks me how I am doing.	☐	☐	☐	☐
4 understand the meaning of "吗" and mark its position in a sentence.	☐	☐	☐	☐
5 read phrases or sentences which have two third tones occurring together.	☐	☐	☐	☐
6 write "你", "我", "他", "大", and "好".	☐	☐	☐	☐

LESSON

3

谢谢你！

Thank You!

My Goals

1 Express gratitude and know how to respond when someone says "Thank you"
2 Extend and respond to an apology
3 Know when to use "不" (no) and what it represents
4 Know that Chinese characters are made up of different components
5 Become familiar with vocabulary associated with showing gratitude and expressing apologies

New Words

谢谢 (xiè xie) thank you	不客气 (bú kè qi) you're welcome

LESSON 3

New Words

duì bu qǐ
对不起 sorry

méi guān xi
没关系 it's fine

TIP

Can you differentiate between "没关系" and "不客气"?

- When someone tells you "对不起", you can say "没关系" to indicate your acceptance of their apology.
- When someone thanks you by saying "谢谢", you can respond humbly by saying "不客气".

xiè xie xiè xie
谢谢你！谢谢他！

qǐng xiè xie tā
请大家谢谢她。

bú yòng xiè bú kè qi
不用谢，不客气！

duì bu qǐ méi guān xi
对不起！没关系！

New Words

qǐng
请 please

tā
她 she; her

bú yòng
不用 no need

Let's Learn GRAMMAR

xiè xie 谢谢

xiè xie
谢谢你！

xiè xie
谢谢他！

xiè xie
谢谢你们！

xiè xie
谢谢他们！

xiè xie
谢谢大家！

TIP

"谢谢" is a common phrase used in conversations.

- If the person whom we wish to thank is in front of us, we can simply say "谢谢".
- When using pronouns such as "他", "你们", and "大家", "谢谢" should precede the pronouns.

bú kè qi 不客气

bú kè qi
不客气！

bú yòng kè qi
不用客气！

qǐng bú yòng kè qi
请不用客气！

TIP

"不客气" and "不用客气" have the same meaning; they are used to respond to an expression of gratitude.

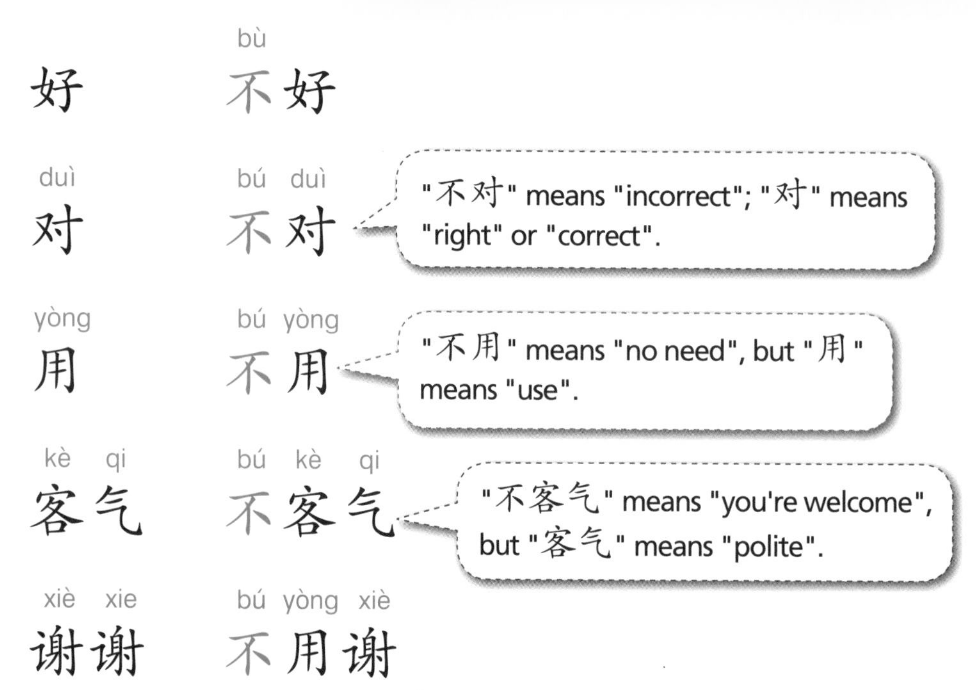

bù
好 不好
duì bú duì
对 不对
"不对" means "incorrect"; "对" means "right" or "correct".
yòng bú yòng
用 不用
"不用" means "no need", but "用" means "use".
kè qi bú kè qi
客气 不客气
"不客气" means "you're welcome", but "客气" means "polite".
xiè xie bú yòng xiè
谢谢 不用谢

Check out the Text > Sentence Pattern section in the Go100 CD.

True or False?

Circle the correct answer.

1. We should talk politely to friends. 对 / 不对
2. When you are sick and people ask you "你好吗？", you should reply "我很好". 对 / 不对
3. When people help us out, we should say "不用谢" to them. 对 / 不对
4. When people say "谢谢" to us, we should reply "不客气". 对 / 不对

Structure of Chinese Characters

Some Chinese characters are composed of two parts written side by side. The left and right components may or may not be in proportion to each other, so study each character carefully before you write them.

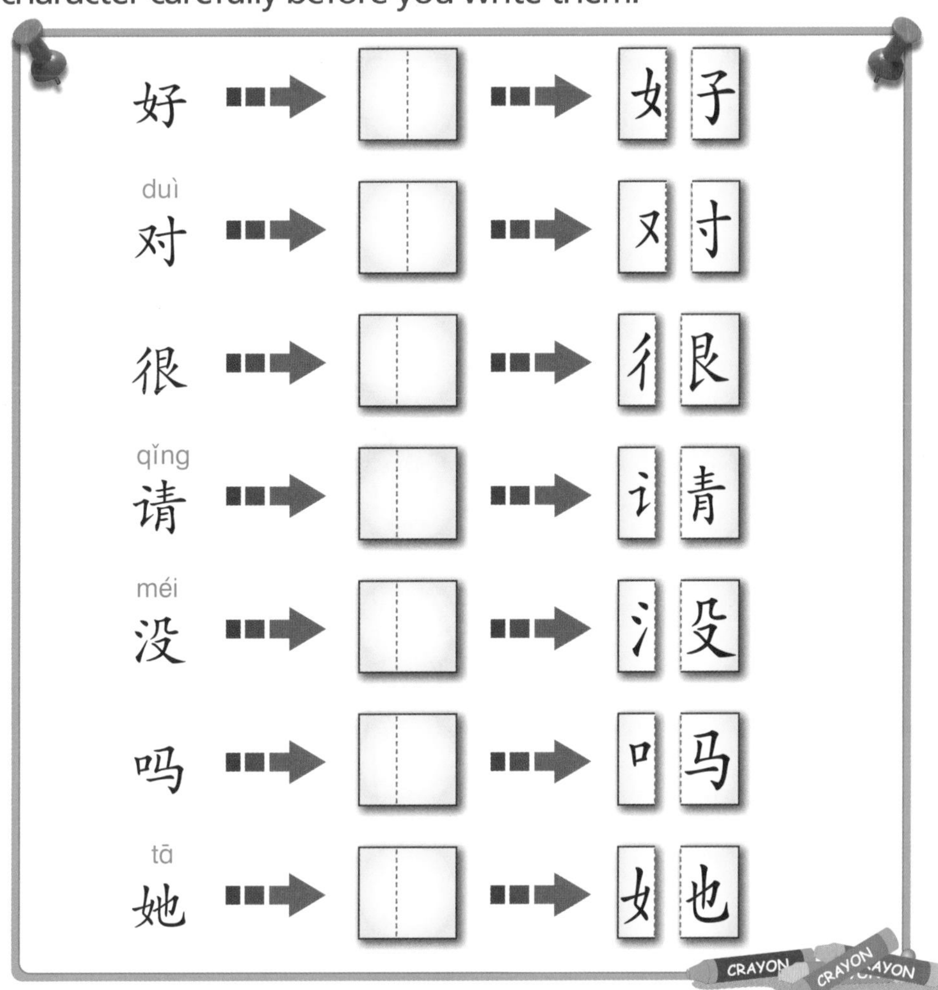

Write out the left and right components of each of the characters below.

1 tā 她 = ☐ + ☐

2 们 = ☐ + ☐

3 好 = ☐ + ☐

4 他 = ☐ + ☐

5 你 = ☐ + ☐

TIP Sometimes, the meaning of a Chinese character may be related to its radical component. Do you know what does "女" or " 亻 " represent when they appear in a character?

→ 女 → 女

→ 人 → 亻

Let's TALK

Find a partner and practice the dialogues below.

Task 1

A: 你好吗？

xiè xie

B: 我很好，谢谢！

Task 2

A: 你早！

B: 你早！

A: 你好吗？

xiè xie

B: 我很好，谢谢你！

qǐng bú yòng kè qi

A: 请不用客气。

Task 3

A: 你好！

B: 你好！

A: Tom 他好吗？

B: Tom 很好。谢谢(xiè xie)！

A: 不客气(bú kè qi)。

Task 4

A: Julie 好吗？

B: 她(tā)很好，谢谢(xiè xie)你！

A: 不用谢(bú yòng xiè)！

Task 5

A: 对不起(duì bu qǐ)！

B: 没关系(méi guān xi)。

Go100

WANT TO LEARN MORE?

Check out the Text > Dialogue section in the Go100 CD.

Let's DO IT

1. How do you show your gratitude or express your apologies in the following situation? Working in pairs, role-play the scenario.

Scenario You accidentally bumped into your classmate along the corridor, causing him to drop the books he was carrying. You helped him pick up the books.

2. Sing a song.

‖1 1 5 5 | 6 6 5 - | 4 4 3 3 | 2 2 1 - |
shuō shuō duì bu qǐ shuō shuō méi guān xi
我说*我说对不起，你说你说没关系。

| 5 5 4 4 | 3 3 2 - | 5 5 4 4 | 3 3 2 - |
shuō shuō xiè xie shuō shuō bú kè qi
你说你说谢谢你，我说我说不客气。

| 1 1 5 5 | 6 6 5 - | 4 4 3 3 | 2 2 1 - ‖
dōu shì péng you dōu shì péng you
大家都是*好朋友，大家都是好朋友。

* 说 say
* 都是 all; both

LEARNING LOG

I can...	Excellent	Good	Fair	Needs Improvement
1 understand the meaning of "谢谢" and "对不起" and use them appropriately.	☐	☐	☐	☐
2 reply "不客气" or "不用客气" when someone says "谢谢" to me.	☐	☐	☐	☐
3 reply "没关系" when someone tells me "对不起".	☐	☐	☐	☐
4 understand that placing "不" before adjectives may create a negative form.	☐	☐	☐	☐
5 identify those Chinese characters that are composed of two parts written side by side, from the new words that I have learnt.	☐	☐	☐	☐
6 write "请", "不", "用", "对", and "没".	☐	☐	☐	☐

LESSON

4

姓什么？

What Is Your Last Name?

qǐng wèn guì xìng
请问你贵姓？
xìng
我姓谢。

My Goals

1. Introduce myself as well as another person
2. Ask for someone's name politely
3. Understand the sequence of Chinese names
4. Become familiar with vocabulary associated with introducing myself and others

Let's READ

qǐng wèn guì xìng
请问你贵姓？
xìng
我姓关。

TIP These are some common Chinese last names. Do you know anyone with any of these last names?

lǐ 李	wáng 王	zhāng 张	liú 刘
chén 陈	yáng 杨	zhào 赵	huáng 黄
xú 徐	zhōu 周	wú 吴	lín 林

qǐng wèn xìng shén me
请问她姓什么？

xìng wáng
她姓王。

New Words

qǐng wèn
请问 may I ask

xìng
姓 last name

guì xìng
贵姓 last name (formal)

shén me
什么 what

wáng
王 (a Chinese last name)

qǐng wèn jiào shén me míng zi
请问他叫什么名字？

jiào wáng xiǎo guì
他叫王小贵。

jiào xiǎo míng
我叫小明，
qǐng wèn jiào shén me míng zi
请问你叫什么名字？

jiào
我叫Billy。

jiào
叫 to call

míng zi
名字 name; first name

xiǎo guì
小贵 (a Chinese name)

xiǎo míng
小明 (a Chinese name)

qǐng wèn guì xìng
你好，请问你贵姓？

de míng zi jiào shén me
你的名字叫什么？

xìng jiào xiǎo míng
我姓谢，叫小明。

dōu jiào xiǎo míng
大家都叫我小明。

New Words

dōu
都 all; already

de
的 (particle before a noun)

Let's Learn GRAMMAR

xìng míng
姓名

míng zi
名字

xìng 姓	míng 名
谢	xiǎo míng 小明
wáng 王	大关

"姓名" means "full name". In Chinese, the last name is followed by the first name.

TIP

Every character has a unique meaning but when it is combined with one or more characters, the meaning may be changed totally. For example, "字" means "character", however, when it comes after "名", the phrase "名字" means "name".

名 (name) + 字 (character) = 名字 (name)

míng zi
名字

shén me míng zi
什么名字？

jiào shén me míng zi
你叫什么名字？

qǐng wèn jiào shén me míng zi
请问你叫什么名字？

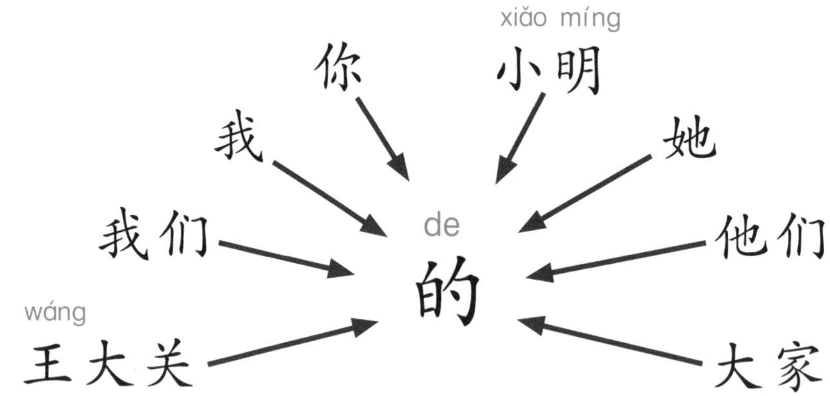

Practice It

Listen to the teacher carefully and follow the instructions.

1 我的(de) 。

2 他的(de) 。

3 你的(de) 。

4 ________的(de) 。

5 ________的(de) 。

6 ________的(de) 。

7 ________的(de) 。

8 ________的(de) 。

9 ________的(de) 。

TIP

The particle "的" can be used to indicate possession. Simply add "的" after the owner (either a name or a personal pronoun) of the object.

shén me
什么

xìng shén me
你姓什么？

xìng shén me
他姓什么？

jiào shén me míng zi
你叫什么名字？

jiào shén me míng zi
他叫什么名字？

TIP
"姓什么" and "叫什么" are both used for asking someone's name.
- "姓什么" → asking for last name of the person
- "叫什么" → asking for first name **or** full name of the person

qǐng wèn
请问

qǐng wèn guì xìng
请问你贵姓？

qǐng wèn jiào shén me míng zi
请问你叫什么名字？

qǐng wèn jiào shén me míng zi
请问他叫什么名字？

TIP
It is more polite if you use "请问" before asking questions.

Check out the Text > Sentence Pattern section in the Go100 CD.

Let's TALK

Find partners to practice the dialogues below.

jiào
我叫Billy。

jiào wáng jiào xiǎo míng
我叫王大关，他叫谢小明。

Task 1

qǐng wèn xìng shén me
A: 请问你姓什么？

jiào shén me míng zi
叫什么名字？

xìng wáng jiào
B: 我姓王，叫大关。

Task 2

xìng shén me
A: 你姓什么？

xìng wáng
B: 我姓王。

xìng shén me
A: 他姓什么？

xìng
B: 他姓谢。

A: 你们好！

B C: 你好！

qǐng wèn guì xìng
A: 请问你贵姓？

xìng
C: 我姓谢。

jiào
A: 我叫Billy，

qǐng wèn jiào shén me míng zi
请问你叫什么名字？

jiào xiǎo míng
C: 我叫小明。

qǐng wèn jiào shén me míng zi
A: 请问他叫什么名字？

jiào wáng
C: 他叫王大关。

Check out the Text > Dialogue section in the Go100 CD.

Let's DO IT

Find partners and practice the dialogue below.
Get them to sign on the chart.

A: 你好！

B: 你好！

A: 请问你贵姓？ (qǐng wèn guì xìng)

B: 我姓 ________ 。 (xìng)

A: 请问你叫什么名字？ (qǐng wèn jiào shén me míng zi)

B: 我叫 ________ 。 (jiào)

LEARNING LOG

I can...	Excellent	Good	Fair	Needs Improvement
1 introduce myself as well as another person.	☐	☐	☐	☐
2 ask for someone's name politely.	☐	☐	☐	☐
3 understand the meaning of the phrase "请问" and use it when I ask questions.	☐	☐	☐	☐
4 use the particle "的" to indicate possession.	☐	☐	☐	☐
5 understand the sequence of Chinese names.	☐	☐	☐	☐
6 write "问", "的", "叫", "名", and "字".	☐	☐	☐	☐

LESSON

5

星期几？ What Day Is Today?

nián yuè

2009 年 9 月

xīng qī rì 星期日	xīng qī yī 星期一	xīng qī èr 星期二	xīng qī sān 星期三	xīng qī sì 星期四	xīng qī wǔ 星期五	xīng qī liù 星期六
		1 Dad's	2	3	4	5
6	7	8 School	9 camp	10	11	12
13	14	15	16	17	18 Swimming	19
20 Ian's	21	22	23	24	Class 25 5p.m.	26
27	28	29	30			

My Goals

1 Learn how to ask or say the date
2 Ask or answer questions relating to quantities and number of days
3 Know the origin of Chinese characters and how they are formed
4 Become familiar with vocabulary associated with talking about dates

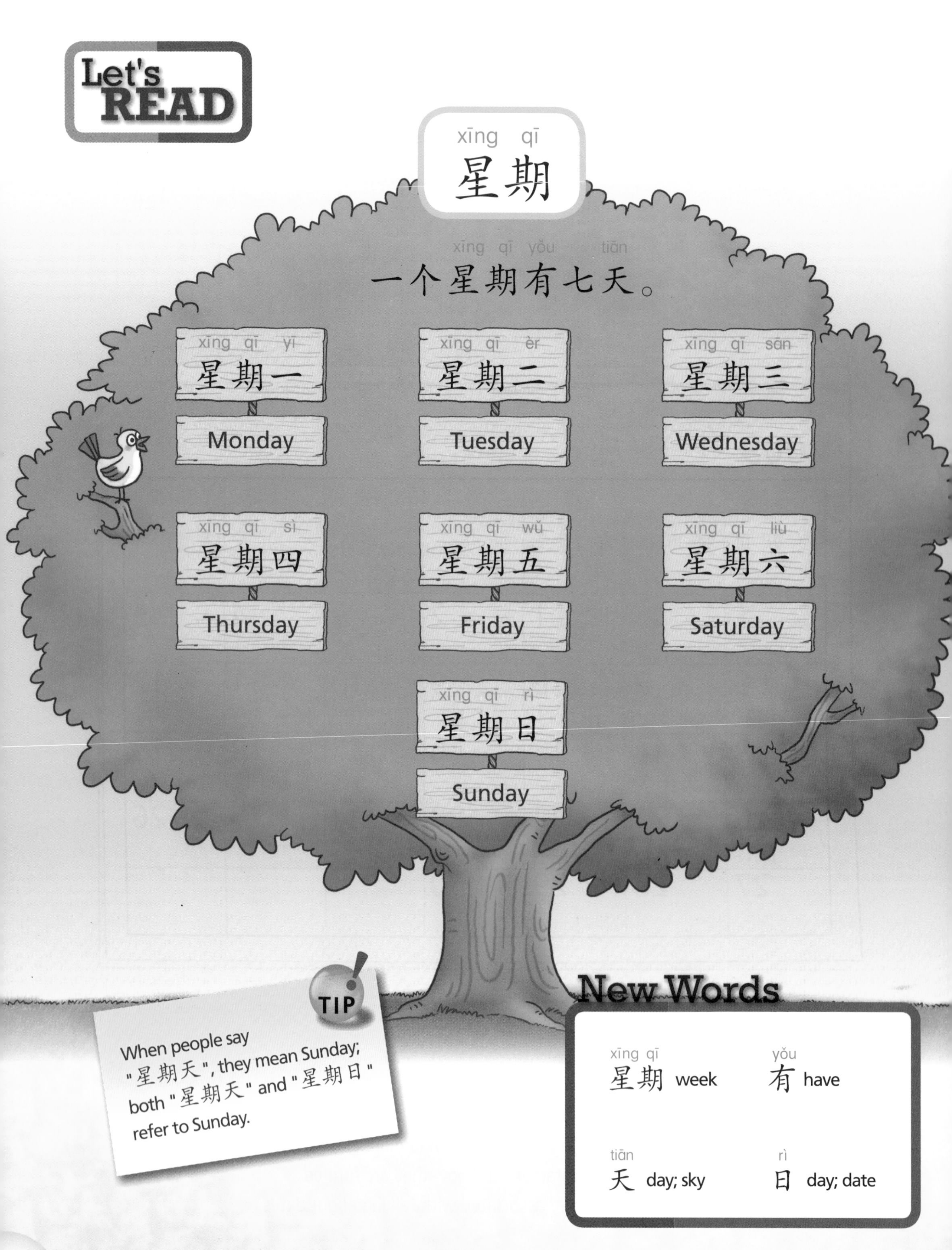
Let's READ
xīng qī
星期
xīng qī yǒu tiān
一个星期有七天。
xīng qī yī
星期一
Monday
xīng qī èr
星期二
Tuesday
xīng qī sān
星期三
Wednesday
xīng qī sì
星期四
Thursday
xīng qī wǔ
星期五
Friday
xīng qī liù
星期六
Saturday
xīng qī rì
星期日
Sunday
TIP
When people say "星期天", they mean Sunday; both "星期天" and "星期日" refer to Sunday.
New Words
xīng qī
星期 week
yǒu
有 have
tiān
天 day; sky
rì
日 day; date

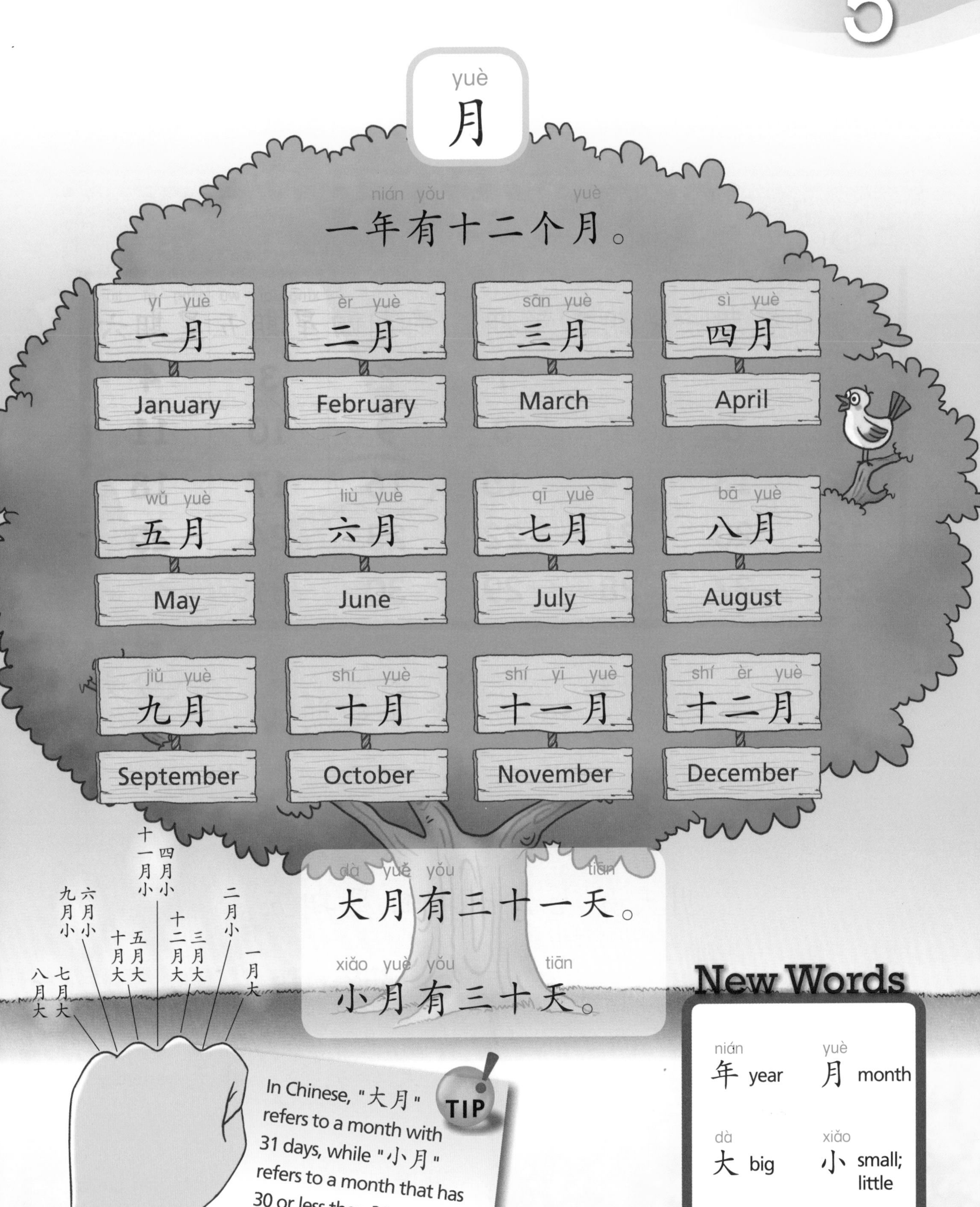

In Chinese, "大月" refers to a month with 31 days, while "小月" refers to a month that has 30 or less than 30 days.

TIP

New Words

nián 年 year	yuè 月 month
dà 大 big	xiǎo 小 small; little

jīn tiān / zuó tiān / míng tiān
今天 / 昨天 / 明天

nián qī yuè
二〇〇九年 七月

xīng qī rì 星期日	xīng qī yī 星期一	xīng qī èr 星期二	xīng qī sān 星期三	xīng qī sì 星期四	星期五	星期六
			1	2	3	4
5	6	7	8	9	10	11
12	13	14	15	16	17	18
19	20	21	22	23	24	25
26	27	28	29	30	31	

今天

jīn tiān shì qī yuè rì xīng qī sì
今天是七月十六日星期四。

zuó tiān shì qī yuè rì xīng qī sān
昨天是七月十五日星期三。

míng tiān shì qī yuè rì xīng qī wǔ
明天是七月十七日星期五。

New Words

jīn tiān 今天 today

zuó tiān 昨天 yesterday

míng tiān 明天 tomorrow

shì 是 to be (am, are, is)

jīn nián qù nián míng nián

今年 / 去年 / 明年

nián	nián	nián
二〇〇八年	二〇〇九年	二〇一〇年

今年 → 二〇〇九年

jīn nián shì nián
今年是二〇〇九年。

qù nián shì nián
去年是二〇〇八年。

míng nián shì nián
明年是二〇一〇年。

TIP

In Chinese, "0" is pronounced as *líng* but is written as "零". However, to indicate years, we usually write the digit "0", for example, 二〇〇八, 二〇〇九.

jīn tiān shì nián yuè rì xīng qī
今天是________年____月____日星期____。

TIP

In Chinese, the basic rule for the sequence of dates is to start from the "biggest" time frame (year) to the "smallest" one (day of the week), for example:

	(day of the week)	(month, day in month)		(year)
	Thursday,	May 14,		2009
Order:	4	2	3	1
Read as:	二〇〇九年	五月	十四日	星期四

New Words

jīn nián
今年 this year

qù nián
去年 last year

míng nián
明年 next year

xīng qī yǒu tiān

一星期，有七天，

xīng qī yī dào xīng qī rì

星期一到星期日，

sì yuè rì xīng qī jǐ

四月十日星期几？

zhè ge yuè yǒu jǐ xīng qī

这个月有几星期？

New Words

dào
到 to arrive

zhè ge
这个 this

jǐ
几 which; how many; a few

Let's Learn GRAMMAR

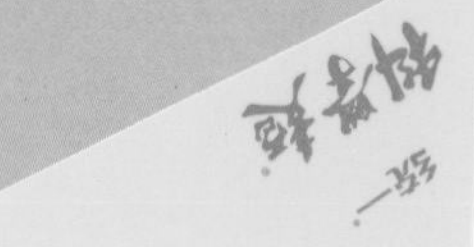

yǒu 有

xīng qī yǒu tiān
一个星期有七天，

sān yuè yǒu tiān
三月有三十一天。

zhè ge yuè yǒu tiān
这个月有三十天。

nián yǒu tiān
一年有三百六十五天。

yǒu bēi zi
我有杯子(cup)。

yǒu shū
Tom 有书(book)。

dào 到

sì yuè rì dào sì yuè rì yǒu tiān
四月一日到四月二十日有二十天。

qī yuè rì dào bā yuè rì yǒu tiān
七月一日到八月三十一日有六十二天。

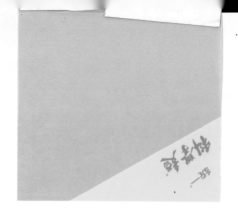

méi yǒu
没有

èr yuè méi yǒu rì
二月没有三十日。

liù yuè méi yǒu rì
六月没有三十一日。

méi yǒu jiě jie
他没有姐姐(sister)。

méi yǒu bēi bāo
我没有背包(backpack)。

zhè ge yuè yǒu jǐ tiān
这个月有几天?

zhè ge yuè yǒu tiān
这个月有三十一天。

zhè ge yuè yǒu jǐ ge xīng qī
这个月有几个星期?

zhè ge zì shì zì
这个字(character)是什么字?

Go100

WANT TO LEARN MORE?

Check out the Text > Sentence Pattern section in the Go100 CD.

Structure of Chinese Characters

Some Chinese characters are composed of two parts written top to bottom. The top and bottom components may or may not be in proportion to each other, so study each character carefully before you write them.

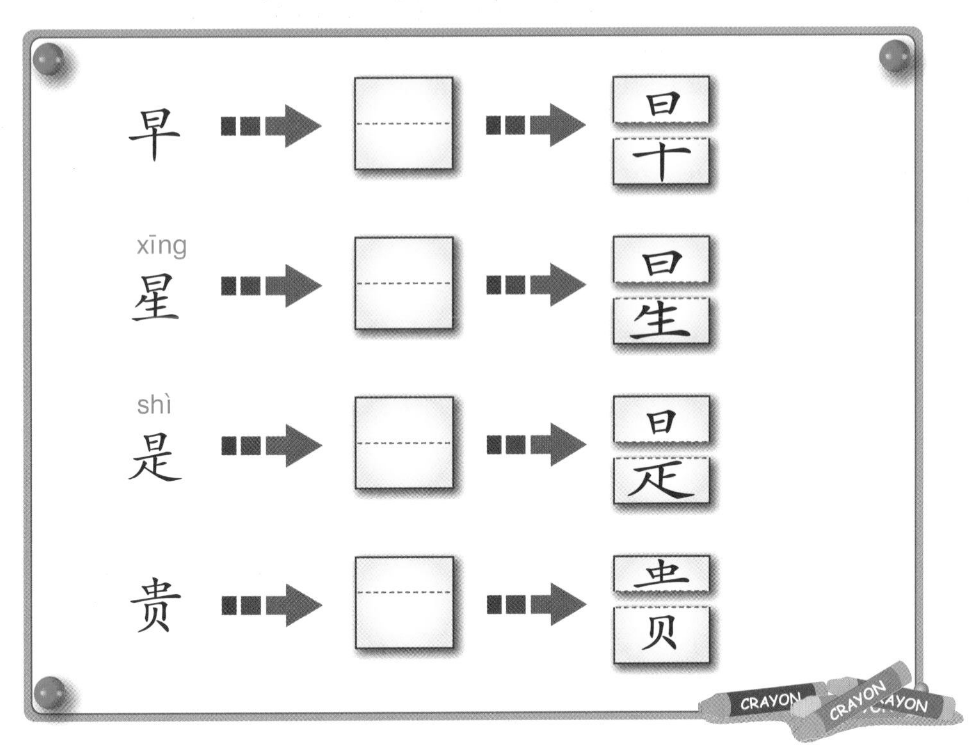

The Origin of Chinese Characters

Many Chinese characters evolved from illustrations. Below are some examples. Can you tell what the illustrations mean? Write the English meaning in the brackets.

1 → 日

(   )

2

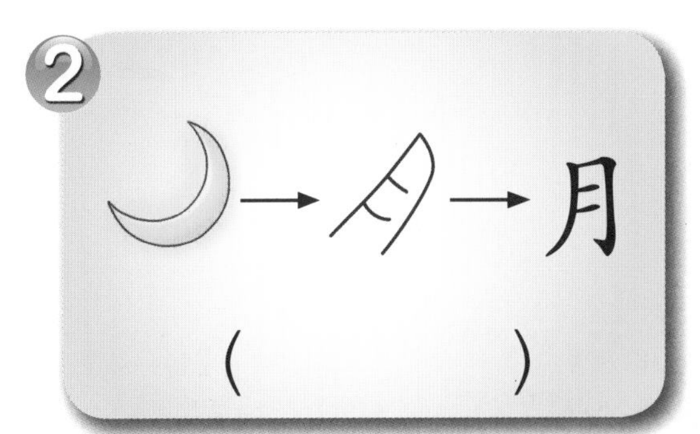

(   )

3

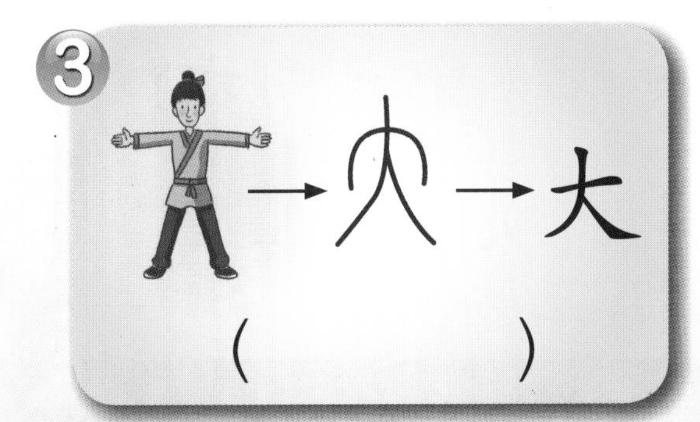

(   )

4 → 星

(   )

Let's TALK

Find a partner and practice the dialogues below.

Task 1

A: 请问右边 (on the right) 有几个橡皮 (eraser)?
(yòu bian ... yǒu jǐ ... xiàng pí)

B: 有四个橡皮。
(yǒu ... xiàng pí)

A: 请问右边有几个字?
(yǒu jǐ ... zì)

B: 有三个字。
(yǒu ... zì)

Task 2

A: 请问一个星期有几天?
(xīng qī yǒu jǐ tiān)

B: 一个星期有 ____ 天。
(xīng qī yǒu ... tiān)

A: 请问八月有几个星期六?
(bā yuè yǒu jǐ ... xīng qī liù)

B: 八月有 ____ 个星期六。
(bā yuè yǒu ... xīng qī liù)

TIP

"几" is a question word for quantity. To answer the question, you need to replace "几" with your answer.

Task 3

zuó tiān shì xīng qī jǐ
A: 请问昨天是星期几？

zuó tiān shì
B: 昨天是 ________________。

jīn tiān shì jǐ yuè jǐ rì
A: 请问今天是几月几日？

jīn tiān shì
B: 今天是 ________________。

míng nián shì jǐ nián
A: 请问明年是几年？

míng nián shì
B: 明年是 ________________。

wǔ yuè rì dào wǔ yuè rì yǒu jǐ tiān
A: 请问五月一日到五月五日有几天？

yǒu
B: 有 ________________。

Go100

WANT TO LEARN MORE?

Check out the Text > Dialogue section in the Go100 CD.

Let's DO IT

shēng rì
"生日" means birthday. Together with five other classmates, practice the dialogue below. Record their birthdays in the table provided.

A: 请问你的生日是几年几月几日？
(shēng rì shì jǐ nián jǐ yuè jǐ rì)

B: 我的生日是____年____月____日。
(shēng rì shì nián yuè rì)

A: 今年的____月____日是星期几？
(jīn nián yuè rì shì xīng qī jǐ)

B: 今年的____月____日是星期____。
(jīn nián yuè rì shì xīng qī)

	Name	Birthday	On which day does the birthday fall on this year?
1			
2			
3			
4			
5			

LEARNING LOG

I can...	Excellent	Good	Fair	Needs Improvement
1 ask about dates politely.	☐	☐	☐	☐
2 talk about dates in Chinese, in the order of year, month, and day.	☐	☐	☐	☐
3 ask and talk about a specific range of days.	☐	☐	☐	☐
4 identify words that are made up of top and bottom components and know that Chinese characters evolved from illustrations.	☐	☐	☐	☐
5 write "有", "月", "天", "今", and "日".	☐	☐	☐	☐

LESSON

6

几口人？

How Many People Are There in Your Family?

My Goals

1 Name family members in Chinese
2 Count and introduce my family members to others
3 Ask someone about his/her family
4 Become familiar with vocabulary associated with introducing family members

mā 妈 mother	bà 爸 father		
gē 哥 older brother	jiě 姐 older sister	mèi 妹 younger sister	dì 弟 younger brother

qǐng wèn nǐ jiā jǐ kǒu rén
请问你家几口人？

bà ba mā ma gē ge jiě jie
爸爸、妈妈、哥哥、姐姐、

dì di mèi mei hái yǒu wǒ
弟弟、妹妹，还有我，

wǒ jiā yí gòng qī kǒu rén
我家一共七口人。

TIP

When introducing or inquiring about the number of family members, the measure word "口" used to be the formal usage. But these days, the measure word "个" is also commonly used. For example, some people may ask, "你家有几个人?"

New Words

jiā 家 home; family	kǒu 口 (a measure word used for counting family members)	rén 人 people; human beings
hái yǒu 还有 still; also; and	yí gòng 一共 in total	

Let's Learn GRAMMAR

有 / 没有

<table>
<tr><td rowspan="2">我</td><td>有</td><td>一个</td><td>gē ge
哥哥。</td></tr>
<tr><td>没有</td><td colspan="2">gē ge
哥哥。</td></tr>
</table>

jiě jie
我有两个姐姐。

mèi mei
你有一个妹妹。

gē ge
我没有哥哥。

mèi mei
他没有妹妹。

jiě jie
他有姐姐。

mèi mei
我没有妹妹。

TIP

"没有" is usually not used together with measure words, so you will never hear people say "我没有两个哥哥" in Chinese.

有……吗？/ 有没有？

你	有	mèi mei 妹妹	吗？
	有没有	mèi mei 妹妹？	

mèi mei
你有妹妹吗？

mèi mei
你有没有妹妹？

"有……吗？" and "有没有？" have the same meaning; they are sentence patterns that indicate a query.

jiě jie
他有姐姐吗？

jiě jie
他有没有姐姐？

一月有三十一日吗？

一月有没有三十一日？

hái yǒu
有……，还有……

我	有	gē ge 哥哥，	hái yǒu 还有	dì di 弟弟。

jiě jie hái yǒu mèi mei
我有姐姐，还有妹妹。

bǐ hái yǒu shū
我有笔(pen)，还有书(book)。

gē ge jiě jie hái yǒu mèi mei
他有一个哥哥、两个姐姐，还有三个妹妹。

yí gòng
一共

jiā yí gòng kǒu rén
他家一共七口人。

jiā yí gòng kǒu rén
我家一共九口人。

yí gòng
七月、八月一共六十二天。

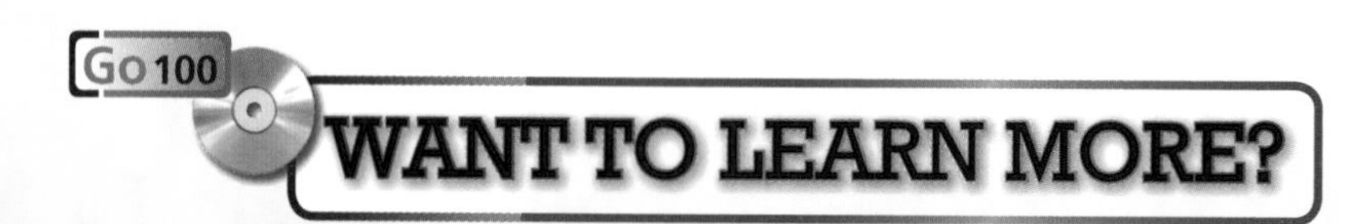

Check out the Text > Sentence Pattern section in the Go100 CD.

Read and Write

Look at the pictures. Then fill in the blanks with the appropriate words.

1. 我家(jiā)有 ______ 口(kǒu)人(rén)，

   我有 ______ 个弟(dì)弟(di)，

   还(hái)有(yǒu) ______ 个妹(mèi)妹(mei)。

2. 我有爸(bà)爸(ba)、______，

   还(hái)有(yǒu)一个 ______。

   我家(jiā)一(yí)共(gòng) ______ 口(kǒu)人(rén)。

3. 我有 ______ 弟(dì)弟(di)，

   ______ 哥(gē)哥(ge)。

   我 ______ 姐(jiě)姐(jie)，______ 妹(mèi)妹(mei)。

Let's TALK

Task 1

Find a partner and practice the dialogue below.

jiā kǒu rén
: 请问你家有几口人？

jiā kǒu rén bà ba mā ma jiě jie hái yǒu
: 我家有四口人，爸爸、妈妈、姐姐，还有我。

gē ge
: 你没有哥哥吗？

gē ge
: 对，我没有哥哥。

gē ge
你有哥哥吗？

gē ge dì di
: 我没有哥哥，我有弟弟。

TIP When answering Yes/No questions in Chinese, we decide if the answer is "对" (yes) or "不对" (no) depending on the accuracy of the question. This is different from English, where we reply according to the correct answer.

In this instance, [girl] does not have a brother. Hence when answering in Chinese, we say "对，我没有哥哥。" In English, however, we will answer "No, I do not have a brother."

Go100

WANT TO LEARN MORE?

Check out the Text > Dialogue section in the Go100 CD.

Task 2

Find a partner and practice the dialogue. Imagine you are  and answer the questions in Chinese.

: 请问你家(jiā)有几口(kǒu)人(rén)？

: 我家(jiā)有 ________。

: 你有没有妹妹(mèi mei)？

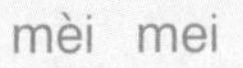

: ________。

: 请问你有弟弟(dì di)吗？

: ________。

: 你弟弟(dì di)叫什么名字？

: 他叫王小星。

Let's DO IT

Bring a family photograph or picture to school. Show it to the class and introduce your family members. You must include the following information in your presentation: the number of people in your family, who they are, and their names.

Write down the family details of three of your classmates in the table below.

名字	jiā kǒu rén 家有几口人？	jiě jie 姐姐	mèi mei 妹妹	gē ge 哥哥	dì di 弟弟
e.g. Adam	五	Ada	-	-	Jack
1					
2					
3					

LEARNING LOG

I can...

		Excellent	Good	Fair	Needs Improvement
1	introduce my family members in Chinese.	☐	☐	☐	☐
2	use "一共" to express a total.	☐	☐	☐	☐
3	use the measure word "口" to indicate the number of family members I have.	☐	☐	☐	☐
4	ask someone about his/her family and the number of family members he/she has.	☐	☐	☐	☐
5	write "口", "人", "爸", "妈", and "还".	☐	☐	☐	☐

My Goals

1. Understand conversations related to buying and selling things
2. Ask questions related to the quantity or price of a product
3. Clearly identify the product I wish to buy
4. Become familiar with vocabulary associated with buying things

Let's READ

New Words

yào
要 need; want

mǎi
买 buy

duō shao
多少 how many; how much

qián
钱 money

kuài
块 (unit of currency)

nà ge duō shao qián
请问那个多少钱？

tài guì le mǎi
太贵了，我不买！

pián yi yì diǎnr
便宜一点儿好不好？

suàn suan duō shao qián
算算一共多少钱？

NEW

pián yi yì diǎnr
便宜一点儿好不好？

TIP

Do you notice the difference in the pinyin for "一点儿 (yì diǎnr)"? "一点儿 (yì diǎnr)" has a special pronunciation; "儿 (er)" is no longer an independent syllable when attached with "点 (diǎn)". Hence when we pronounce "一点儿 (yì diǎnr)", we have to raise the tip of our tongue and curl back over the tongue itself when saying the word "点 (diǎn)".

New Words

nà ge 那个 that	guì 贵 expensive	tài guì le 太贵了 too expensive
pián yi 便宜 cheap	yì diǎnr 一点儿 a little bit	suàn 算 to calculate or count

Let's Learn GRAMMAR

这个 / 那个 (nà ge)

这个九块钱 (kuài qián)，
那个 (nà ge) 十块钱 (kuài qián)，
一共十九块钱 (kuài qián)。

请问这个多少钱 (duō shao qián)？
请问那个 (nà ge) 多少钱 (duō shao qián)？

我要买苹果 (yào mǎi píng guǒ) (apple)，
请问苹果多少钱 (píng guǒ duō shao qián)？

pián yi / guì
便宜 / 贵

pián yi 便宜 ⟷ guì 贵

kuài	kuài	kuài	kuài	kuài
40 块	85 块	100 块	200 块	400 块

pián yi 很便宜　pián yi 便宜

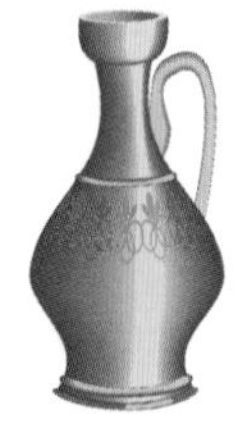

guì 贵　guì 很贵

很

pián yi 很便宜　guì 很贵

很小　很大

shǎo 很少　duō 很多

TIP

"很" means "very". It is an adverb of degree which goes before adjectives or verbs.

---

shǎo duō
少 / 多

shǎo 少 ⟷ duō 多

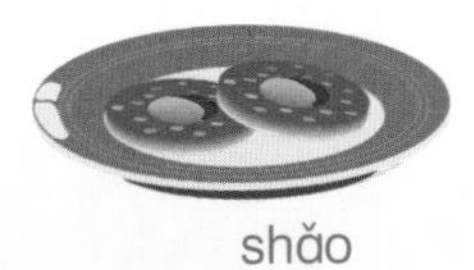

shǎo 很少　shǎo 少　duō 多　duō 很多

yào yào
要 / 要……吗？

yào mǎi
A：请问你要买什么？

yào mǎi pū mǎn
B：我要买五个扑满(piggy bank)。

yào mǎi qún zi
A：你要买裙子(skirt)吗？

mǎi qún zi yào mǎi xié zi
B：我不买裙子，我要买鞋子(shoes)。

yào mǎi
A：请问你要买这个吗？

mǎi
B：我不买，谢谢。

几 / 多少 (duō shao)

你有几个姐姐？

一个星期有几天？

你家有几口人？

TIP

When asking questions related to quantity,
- "几" usually applies to numbers below 10.
- "多少" applies to any other number.
- use "多少" if you are unable to estimate the quantity.

When asking about one's age,
- "你几岁？" is used when we talk to children 10 years old or younger.
- "你多大？" is used when we talk to people of the same age. It can also be used when talking to children of any age.
- "您(nín)多大年纪(nián jì)？" is used when we talk to people who are older than us.

A: 你几岁(suì)？

B: 我八岁(suì)。

A: 他几岁(suì)？

B: 他十岁(suì)。

这个多少钱(duō shao qián)？

那个(nà ge)多少钱(duō shao qián)？

十月有多少(duō shao)天？

一年有多少(duō shao)天？

New Words

岁 (suì) years of age (a measure word)

Go100 WANT TO LEARN MORE?

Check out the Text > Sentence Pattern section in the Go100 CD.

Let's TALK

Find a partner and practice the dialogues below.

Task 1

yào mǎi
A：请问你要买什么？

yào mǎi duō shao qián
B：我要买这个，请问这个多少钱？

kuài
A：这个10块。

yào mǎi
B：我要买两个，

suàn suan duō shao qián
算算一共多少钱？

kuài
A：两个一共20块。

Go100

WANT TO LEARN MORE?

Check out the Text > Dialogue section in the Go100 CD.

Task 2

yào mǎi
A: 请问你要买什么？

yào mǎi duō shao qián
B: 我要买这个，请问这个多少钱？

kuài
A: 这个27块。

kuài tài guì le pián yi yì diǎnr
B: 27块太贵了，便宜一点儿好不好？

mǎi nà ge
A: 你买那个好吗？

nà ge kuài pián yi
那个13块，很便宜。

kuài pián yi yào mǎi
B: 13块很便宜，我要买两个。

Want More Practice?

Replace the red text with the items below:

kuài
39 块

kuài
8 块

kuài
99 块

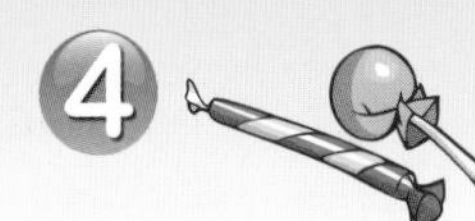

kuài
2 块

Let's DO IT

Work in pairs. One of you will pretend to be a stall owner while the other will act as a customer.

Using the vocabulary and sentence patterns you have just learned, the "stall owner" must find out what the "customer" wants to buy and calculate the total cost of the purchase. The "customer" may try to bargain with the "stall owner" for a better price if he/she feels that the item is too expensive. Write down your transaction details in the table below.

Item	List Price	Quantity	Discounted Price	Subtotal
			Total:	

LEARNING LOG

I can...

		Excellent	Good	Fair	Needs Improvement
1	use "要" and "要……吗?" to say what I want to buy and ask others what they want to purchase.	☐	☐	☐	☐
2	use "……块 (钱)" to name the price of an item.	☐	☐	☐	☐
3	ask about the price and quantity of an item.	☐	☐	☐	☐
4	use "便宜" and "贵" to express what I think about an item's price.	☐	☐	☐	☐
5	express the intensity of something by adding the adverb of degree "很" before the adjective.	☐	☐	☐	☐
6	write "要", "买", "多", "少", and "了".	☐	☐	☐	☐

LESSON

8

几点钟？

What Time Is It?

My Goals

1. Ask someone for the time
2. Tell time in Chinese
3. Ask or say if a person is at a specific location at a particular time
4. Become familiar with vocabulary associated with telling time

Let's READ

1

diǎn
三点

2

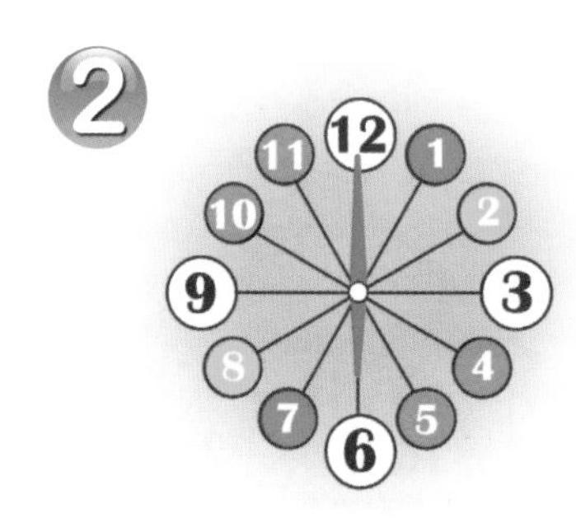

diǎn
六点

3

diǎn
八点

4

diǎn bàn
三点半

5

diǎn bàn
十点半

6

diǎn bàn
七点半

TIP
bàn
"半" means half.
Cut a cake into half.
1 hour is 60 minutes,
half of 60 minutes is
30 minutes.
chī bàn
一个人吃(eat)半个
dàn gāo
蛋糕(cake)。
diǎn fēn diǎn bàn
七点三十分 = 七点半

New Words

diǎn
点 o'clock (indicating time of day)

bàn
半 half

diǎn fēn
一点三十五分

diǎn fēn
三点四十分

diǎn fēn
六点五十分

diǎn fēn
十二点十分

diǎn fēn
五点十五分

diǎn fēn
九点二十五分

New Words

fēn
分 minute

xiàn zài diǎn zhōng
现在几点钟？

xiàn zài shàng wǔ diǎn zhōng
现在上午九点钟。

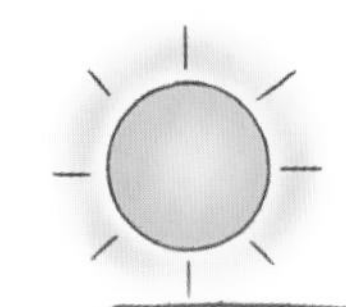

TIP

When "……点钟" is used to refer to "o' clock", "钟" can be omitted.

xiàn zài diǎn
请问现在几点？

xiàn zài zhōng wǔ diǎn fēn
现在中午十二点三十五分。

zài
你爸爸今天在家吗？

zài
我爸爸今天不在家，
wǎn shang zài
他明天晚上在家。

New Words

zài 在 in	xiàn zài 现在 now	diǎn zhōng ……点钟 o'clock (indicating time of day)
shàng wǔ 上午 morning	zhōng wǔ 中午 noon	wǎn shang 晚上 night

xiàn zài diǎn zhōng
请问现在几点钟？

xià wǔ diǎn fēn
下午三点五十分，

fēn diǎn zhōng
还有十分四点钟，

diǎn bàn shí zǒu
四点半时我要走。

New Words

xià wǔ
下午 afternoon

shí
时 time; when

zǒu
走 depart; walk; leave

Let's Learn GRAMMAR

zài 在 / zài 不在

他	zài 在	家。
	zài 不在	

zài
小明在家。

zài
姐姐不在家。

zài
小明的爸爸不在家。

zài
小明的妈妈在家。

xià wǔ diǎn zài
我下午三点在家。

wǎn shang diǎn zài
我晚上十点不在家。

TIP

In Chinese, dates and times are generally sequenced "from big to small" (in other words, from general to specific).
For example:

	July	26,	2009
Order:	2	3	1
Read as:	二〇〇九年	七月	二十六日

	9:	14	p.m.	8:	34	a.m.
Order:	2	3	1	2	3	1
Read as:	晚上	9点	14分	上午	8点	34分

zài 在……吗？ / zài 在不在？

你	zài 在	家	吗？
	zài zài 在不在		？

zài
明天你在家吗？

zài zài
明天你在不在家？

zài xué xiào
星期二你在学校(school)吗？

zài zài xué xiào
星期二你在不在学校？

xià wǔ zài
星期日下午你哥哥在家吗？

xià wǔ zài zài
星期日下午你哥哥在不在家？

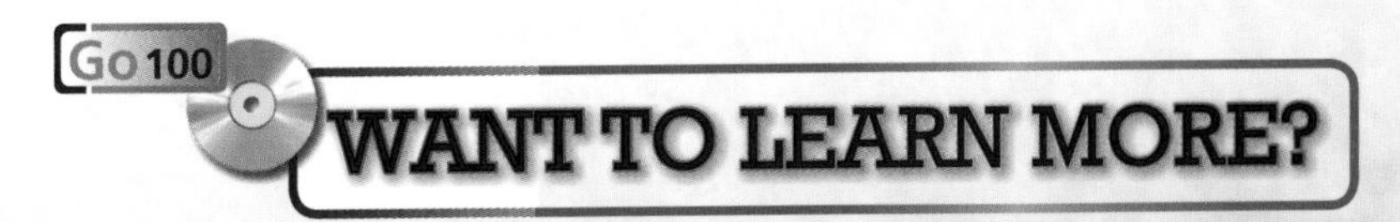

Check out the Text > Sentence Pattern section in the Go100 CD.

Find a partner and practice the dialogues below.

Task 1

A: 请问明天你在(zài)家吗？

B: 明天上午(shàng wǔ)我在(zài)家。

明天下午(xià wǔ)我不在(zài)家。

Task 2

A: 请问现在(xiàn zài)几点钟(diǎn zhōng)？

B: 还有十分钟(fēn zhōng)九点(diǎn)，

你几点(diǎn)要走(zǒu)？

A: 我九点(diǎn)半(bàn)要走(zǒu)。

New Words

fēn zhōng
分钟 minute

Go100

WANT TO LEARN MORE?

Check out the Text > Dialogue section in the Go100 CD.

Task 3

Look at the pictures and answer the questions in Chinese.

1

xiàn zài diǎn zhōng
A: 请问现在几点钟？

B: ______________________。

2

fēn zhōng diǎn
A: 还有十分钟十二点，
xiàn zài diǎn zhōng
请问现在几点钟？

B: ______________________。

3

TV9 Program

12:30 p.m. :	News
1:00 p.m. :	Decorating Your Home
1:30 p.m. :	Drama (Ep. 3)
3:15 p.m. :	Tomato Man
4:45 p.m. :	E-Buzz

A: 请问Tomato Man
diǎn kāi shǐ
几点开始(start)？

B: ______________________。

4

wǎn shang
A: 请问星期三晚上七
diǎn bàn zài
点半，你在家吗？

B: ______________________。

Let's DO IT

1 Look at the table below and answer the questions in Chinese.

Adam's day schedule	
8:00a.m.-12:00p.m.	Attend classes at school
12:00p.m.-2:00p.m.	Study at the library
2:00p.m.-3:30p.m.	Piano lesson
3:30p.m.-6:30p.m.	Home
6:30p.m.-8:00p.m.	Concert
8:00p.m.	Return home

xià wǔ diǎn bàn zài

1. Adam下午两点半在家吗？ ______________________________

wǎn shang diǎn zhōng zài zài

2. 他晚上九点钟在不在家？ ______________________________

2 Your friend has just bought a new game console and has invited you over to his home to play together. You need to arrange a convenient day and time to pay him a visit. Working in pairs, role-play the scenario.

LEARNING LOG

I can...	Excellent	Good	Fair	Needs Improvement
1 ask for the time in Chinese.	☐	☐	☐	☐
2 tell time accurately and use "上午", "中午", "下午", and "晚上" appropriately.	☐	☐	☐	☐
3 express "one hour" and "half an hour" in Chinese.	☐	☐	☐	☐
4 use "在" to ask or say if a person is at a specific location at a particular time.	☐	☐	☐	☐
5 write "上", "中", "下", "在", and "走".	☐	☐	☐	☐

LESSON

9

打电话

Making a Phone Call

你好！

zhǎo shéi
你好，请问你找谁？

My Goals

1. Make and answer telephone calls in Chinese
2. Inquire about and tell the telephone number
3. Know the difference between English and Chinese telephone terminology
4. Become familiar with basic vocabulary associated with making and answering telephone calls

Let's READ

你好！

zhǎo shéi
你好，请问你找谁？

zhǎo
我找谢小明。

谢小明不在家。

dǎ diàn huà zhǎo
我明天再打电话找他。

好，再见！

再见！

TIP Chinese people do not usually identify themselves when answering or making a phone call. If they do, they will say "我是Mary". Literally, this means "I am Mary", which is equivalent to "This is Mary speaking."

New Words

zhǎo
找 to look for; to find

shéi
谁 who; whom

dǎ diàn huà
打电话 to make a phone call

zhǎo nǎ wèi
请问你找哪一位？

diàn huà hào
你的电话多少号？

děng yi děng lái
等一等，我来了！

shéi dǎ diàn huà zhǎo
是谁打电话找我？

TIP

There are many ways to ask for telephone numbers. "你的电话是几号？" is very commonly used too.

New Words

nǎ 哪 which; what	wèi 位 (a measure word for people)	hào 号 number
děng yi děng 等一等 wait a moment	lái 来 to come	

Let's Learn GRAMMAR

shéi
谁

shéi
谁的？

shéi
这是谁的？

shéi
这是谁的家？

shéi zhǎo
谁找我？

shéi
谁有钱？

shéi dǎ diàn huà
谁在打电话？

shéi
谁？

zhǎo shéi
你找谁？

zhǎo shéi
请问你找谁？

TIP Both "谁" and "什么" are question words. We use "谁" when asking about people. However, when asking about objects, we use "什么". Note that "谁" can also be used independently.

Compare It

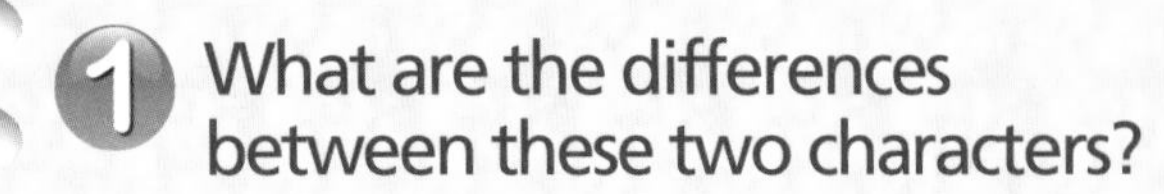

1. What are the differences between these two characters?

2. What are the similarities between these two characters?

扌+戈=找

扌+丁=打

zhǎo
找

zhǎo
哥哥，有人找你。

A：请问你找谁？(zhǎo shéi)

B：我找谢小明。(zhǎo)

A：你找我哥哥吗？(zhǎo)

B：对，我找你哥哥。(zhǎo)

Compare It

3 Compare the red components on the left and the right. How are they different?

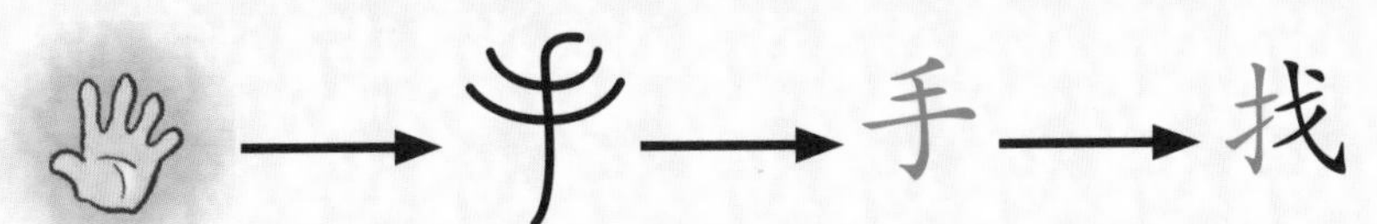

→ → 口 → 哪

→ → 女 → 妈

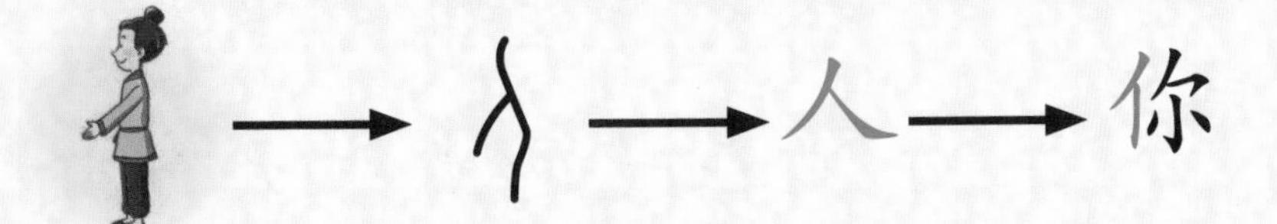

TIP When a Chinese character combines with another component to form a new word, its form and shape may be modified.

是 / 不是

他	是	小明的哥哥。
	不是	

你是大关的姐姐。

不是，我不是大关的姐姐。

现在不是三点半，现在是四点半。

明天不是星期一，明天是星期二。

是……吗？

他	是	谢小明	吗？

你是小明的弟弟吗？

今天是星期五吗？

现在是两点十五分吗？

dĕng yí xià dĕng yi dĕng dĕng
等一下 / 等一等 / 等

dĕng yí xià
请你等一下。

dĕng yi dĕng
请你等一等。

dĕng
请你等十分钟。

dĕng
请你再等五分钟。

dĕng
我们等你。

TIP

"等一下" and "等一等" are used when you need someone to wait for a short period. They cannot be followed by any mention of a specific time or the person whom one is waiting for. To talk about a specific waiting period or person, we simply use "等".

nǎ
那 / 哪

wèi
那位是小明的爸爸。

nǎ wèi
哪一位是小明的爸爸？

那个是我的电话。

nǎ
哪一个是你的电话？

TIP

"那" and "哪" have different usages. In this instance, "那(一个)" refers to "that one"; the target or object is certain. It is usually used in declarative sentences. "哪(一个)" has the meaning of "which one" and is usually used in interrogative sentences.

Go100

WANT TO LEARN MORE?

Check out the Text > Sentence Pattern section in the Go100 CD.

Let's TALK

Find a partner and practice the dialogues below.

Task 1

A: 请问你找(zhǎo)哪(nǎ)一位(wèi)?

B: 我找(zhǎo)谢小明。

A: 好，请你等(děng)一(yí)下(xià)。

B: 谢谢！

Task 2

A: 请问你找(zhǎo)哪(nǎ)一位(wèi)?

B: 我找(zhǎo)小明的爸爸。

A: 他不在家。

Task 3

A: 你好，请问你找(zhǎo)谁(shéi)?

B: 我找(zhǎo)大关。

A: 对不起，大关不在家。

Go100 **WANT TO LEARN MORE?**

Check out the Text > Dialogue section in the Go100 CD.

Task 4

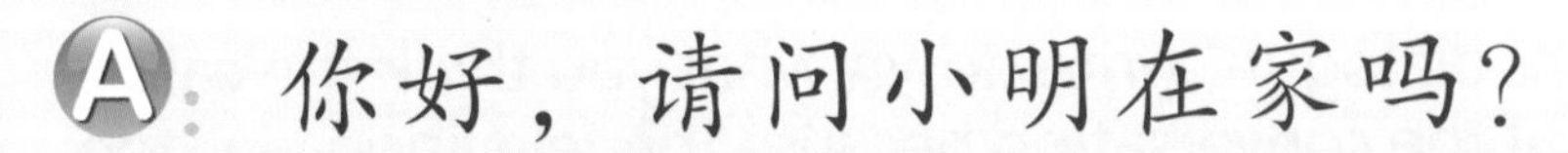

A: 你好，请问小明在家吗？

dĕng yí xià

B: 请你等一下。

dă diàn huà zhăo

哥哥，有人打电话找你。

Task 5

zhăo

A: 你好，我是小明，我要找大关。

B: 对不起，大关不在家。

A: 明天他在家吗？

B: 明天他在家。

dă diàn huà zhăo

A: 明天我再打电话找他。

Task 6

diàn huà hào

A: 请问你家电话多少号？

diàn huà

B: 我家电话是27507631。

Let's DO IT

It is 5:00p.m. on a Wednesday. You are watching television with your brother when the telephone rings. Your brother answers the call.

1 Group discussion

Based on clues from your brother's dialogue, write down what you think the caller is saying. You missed some parts of the conversation because the television was too loud. Discuss with your group members and complete your brother's dialogue.

These key phrases may be useful in your discussion:

哥哥 / 妈妈 / 爸爸 / 弟弟　　现在 / 早上 / 下午 / 早一点儿 / 晚一点儿
下午四点钟 / 下午六点钟 / 早上十点钟 / 中午十二点钟
我是…… /你是…… /他是…… /朋友

哥哥：你好！请问你找哪一位？
caller:
哥哥：她现在不在家，请你(____________)再打来。
caller:
哥哥：现在下午五点钟，请你(____________)再打来。
caller:
哥哥：请问你是哪一位？
caller:
哥哥：再见。

2 After completing the conversation, find a partner and role-play the scenario. Take turns to play the role of the brother and the caller.

LEARNING LOG

I can...	Excellent	Good	Fair	Needs Improvement
1 ask the caller who he/she is looking for as well as say who I am looking for in a phone conversation.	☐	☐	☐	☐
2 respond appropriately after the caller identifies who he/she is looking for.	☐	☐	☐	☐
3 inquire about and tell the telephone number.	☐	☐	☐	☐
4 tell the difference between "那" and "哪".	☐	☐	☐	☐
5 write "找", "谁", "打", "话", and "来".	☐	☐	☐	☐

LESSON

10 好老师 A Good Teacher

My Goals

1 Be able to ask about or say the things I (or others) know about
2 Be able to ask about or say the things I (or others) can do
3 Know how to address the teacher in Chinese
4 Learn vocabulary associated with expressing my abilities

Let's READ

lǎo shī
老师好！

tóng xué
同学好！

lǎo shī
我是王老师，

jiāo zhōng wén
今天教你们中文，

yì qǐ xué zhōng wén
我们一起学中文。

TIP How do you address your teachers? Chinese people address their teachers as "(teacher's last name) + 老师", for example, "王老师". This is different from "Mr. Wang" or "Ms. Wang" in English, which in Chinese means "王先生" and "王小姐" respectively.

New Words

lǎo shī 老师 teacher	xué 学 to learn	tóng xué 同学 classmate
jiāo 教 to teach	zhōng wén 中文 Chinese	yì qǐ 一起 together

jiāo
教

xué
学

lǎo shī jiāo
老师教我。

lǎo shī jiāo zhōng wén
老师教我中文。

lǎo shī jiāo xué zhōng wén
老师教我学中文。

xué zhōng wén
我学中文。

xué zhōng wén
我们学中文。

yì qǐ xué zhōng wén
我们一起学中文。

lǎo shī jiāo zhōng wén
老师教我们中文。

lǎo shī jiāo xué zhōng wén
老师教我们学中文。

lǎo shī jiāo xué zhōng wén
谢谢老师教我们学中文。

xué sheng xué zhōng wén yǒu yòng
学生：学中文有用吗？

lǎo shī xué zhōng wén yǒu yòng
老师：学中文很有用。

New Words

xué sheng
学生 student; pupil

yǒu yòng
有用 useful

lǎo shī tóng xué
老师好，同学好。

lǎo shī jiāo xué zhōng wén
老师教我学中文。

hé tóng xué yì qǐ xué
我和同学一起学，

huì kě yǐ lǎo shī
不会可以问老师。

New Words

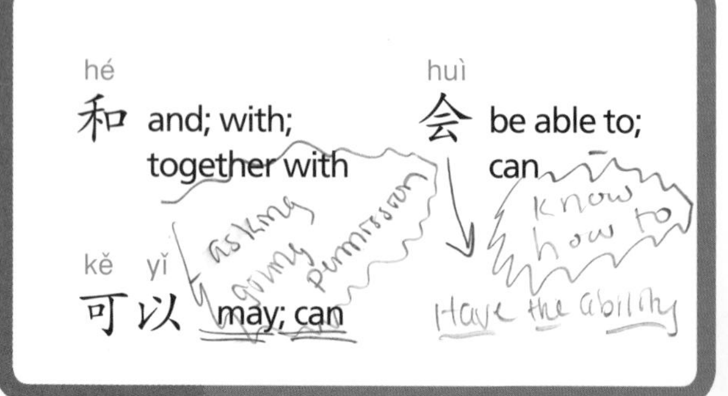

hé
和 and; with; together with

huì
会 be able to; can

kě yǐ
可以 may; can